MIND OVER TENNIS

Mastering the Mental Game

MIND OVER TENNIS

Mastering the Mental Game

Jörgen Jensen
with Peter Lundgren

Accomplishing
Innovation Press

Mind Over Tennis: Mastering the Mental Game
Copyright © 2021 Jörgen Jensen with Peter Lundgren. All rights reserved.

Address
Sickla Sjöväg 4
131 33 Nacka,
Sweden

www.mindovertennis.com

Accomplishing Innovation Press
1497 Main St. Suite 169
Dunedin, FL 34698
4horsemenpublications.com
AccomplishingInnovationPress@gmail.com

Cover by: Jenn Kotick
Typesetting by MC
Editor Shelley Sand

All rights to the work within are reserved to the author and publisher. No part of this publication may be reproduced, stored in a retrieval system, or transmitted in any form or by any means, electronic, mechanical, photocopying, recording, scanning, or otherwise, except as permitted under Section 107 or 108 of the 1976 International Copyright Act, without prior written permission except in brief quotations embodied in critical articles and reviews. Please contact either the Publisher or Author to gain permission.

This book is meant as a reference guide. All characters, organizations, and events portrayed in this novel are either products of the author's imagination or are used fictitiously. All brands, quotes, and cited work respectfully belong to the original rights holders and bear no affiliation to the authors or publisher.

Library of Congress Control Number: 2021951200

Paperback ISBN-13: 978-1-64450-452-9
Ebook ISBN-13: 978-1-64450-451-2

CONTENTS

Preface and Acknowledgements vii
Playing in the Zone 1
The Importance of Preparation and Knowledge 11
Peter: Baptism by fire (the Marcelo Rios story) 21
Peter: Raising Genius (and wrestling Federer) 25

PART TWO
Effective Training Quantity or Quality? 35
Understanding the Principles of Training 42
Structure and Planning. 52
Peter: A Fiery Time with a Fiery Player 59
Match Analysis and Planning 65
The Master Coach 69
The Importance of Consistency 77
Consistency Training 85
About Feeds 95
Peter: Neglected skills 98
Peter: The Impenetrable Castle (Björn Borg) 100

PART THREE
Understanding Emotions 106
Peter: Mental Meltdown 120
Dealing with Unwanted Emotions 121
Change Your Attitude to Yourself. 129
Re-framing 132
Deep Analysis— Getting to the Source 135
Willpower Training 138
Peter's method at critical points 142
Be Prepared to Double up 145
Concentration Drill 149
Visualization 151
Converting Negative Energy to Positive 154
Bad Days 156
Peter: Wawrinka vs Federer 160
Reaching the Zone 164
Acknowledgements 168

PREFACE

Before diving into the heat of the action, I would like to briefly introduce the authors and explain a bit about how the book came about, how the content is organized, what subjects are covered and also acknowledge people who have helped with the book.

PETER LUNDGREN *is a name familiar to most people in the tennis world. A brief introduction might nonetheless be in order. Peter, an accomplished tennis player in his own right (reached as high as 25 in the world rankings), is perhaps best known for his role as coach and mentor of Roger Federer in the beginning of Roger's incredible career, and before he became the one and only ROGER FEDERER. Prior to taking on Federer, Peter had worked with Marcelo Rios, who was known by all as a most formidable—if not impossible—challenge to coach. Other coaches had given up, but Lundgren kept at it for close to a year (after which he is reported to have said "What Ríos needs is not a coach, but a psychologist"). Still, Ríos reached as far as world number one, and this in no small measure thanks to the efforts of Lundgren. Despite splitting up with Ríos, Lundgren had apparently impressed the tennis world enough with his coaching skills that the Swiss Federation asked for his help. They particularly wanted help with a 16-year-old player, who on one hand was very talented, but on the other hand risked wasting his talent due to his hot temper and bad behavior. His name? Roger Federer.*

As we all know, the partnership turned out pretty successful, and Peter managed to help Federer grow, from an ill-tempered teen to the consummate professional we have come to love. This is what Roger had to say in an interview in 2003, about his transformation under Lundgren's mentorship. *"Before, I* would throw my racquet, curse and I did not like to train. Max one and a half hour, and then I had enough." A few years later Federer had won his first Wimbledon and become the number one ranked player in the world.

After splitting up with Federer, Lundgren continued coaching and took on Marat Safin. In the 2005 Australian Open Safin and Federer met in the singles semi-finals. Federer was the defending champion and the number one player in the world. This is what one newspaper in Sweden had to say about it:

> "Rios, Federer and Marat Safin are all players who have needed both a coach and a psychologist, and with Lundgren they have encountered both. He makes his players feel well and happy, and a player who feels good plays good. Like Safin yesterday. The Russian, who previously should have been made to wear a straight jacket at side change, kept his composure in the nail-biter match against Federer, and if he had not succeeded with this he would never have beaten him. When Safin in the spring of 2004 hired Peter Lundgren as a coach he was off balance as a player, and had fallen to a ranking of 23. After beating Federer in the semis he will now be playing in the finals in Australian Open on Sunday. Probably the only one who believed Safin could pull this off was Lundgren."

(Aftonbladet 28 Jan 2005)

I personally met Peter for the first time in the summer of 2017. I was coaching a young Swedish talent, Mikael Ymer, at the time, and we had decided to add some more coaching expertise to our team. Peter and I immediately hit it off. But then again, who would not get along well with Peter? We thought very similarly about the game, coaching and the mental aspects. I was therefore very happy when Peter generously agreed to partake in this book project. Peter possesses, in my opinion, many of the very key characteristics that define a good coach. Additionally, he is a virtual treasure chest of interesting and informative stories and anecdotes from his own career as a coach and player. And, incidentally, when he was young he was a training partner with Bjorn Borg, and got to see close-up how Bjorn trained, thought, and approached the game. What better source of learning the mental game could you possibly ask for?

And how about myself? I do not have a career as a player on the ATP tour. What I do have is about a 40-year record coaching and teaching. My experience has mostly involved mental coaching in various forms, both in tennis and in other activities. In addition to that I have worked in the school world as a teacher and principal, where I learned a lot about dealing with parents and how to speed up learning in various ways. One research project that I conducted dealt with the subject of acquiring physical skills in the fastest, most effective way (this proved very workable in tennis, especially when it came to building consistency). I have coached tennis players of all levels, from the very top ATP level all the way down to recreational.

So why another book on the mental game of tennis?

Mental coaching and sports psychology in general tend to focus mostly on handling the various difficulties players run into when competing (such as nervousness or anger issues, etc.). My view is that this is quite a limited perspective of what it takes to be a top performer. To give just a few examples: goal setting and structure affect mental performance. Strategy and tactics are certainly mental abilities, too, but are rarely covered within the constraints of the traditional approach to sports psychology. Training and practice routines also have a lot to do with mental factors. Last but not least: the aspect of how to rise to the very highest levels of performance, sometimes called "The Zone," is a most important subject only sparingly covered elsewhere.

My purpose with this book is to fill these gaps.

While working on this book I have met with many of the best coaches and players in the world. It turns out that they often have figured out workable approaches to improve on their players' mental game (or their own, during the time when they were actively competing). I worked in close association with Good to Great tennis academy in Stockholm for several years, and the coaches and players there were kind enough to let me interview them about their own experiences and successful methods in the field of mental tennis. I am especially grateful for the participation of Magnus Norman, who was named best coach in the world 2016.

The book is organized so that the content of some chapters is of a more "technical" nature, while others are real-life examples and anecdotes, mostly from the illustrious career of Peter Lundgren. When trying to improve the mental game there are two approaches that work, and both of them are necessary for success. One is practical advice ("so how do I actually do this?"). The other is a theoretical understanding of how things work "under the hood" so to speak. Without the understanding, the practical drills become less effective. Conversely, with only theory and no drills little to nothing practical ever comes about.

I hope this book will help the reader become more proficient in the mental game, and as a result will find that he or she has achieved a state of "Mind over Tennis".

Left to right: Peter Lundgren, Elias Ymer, Mikael Ymer, Robin Söderling, Jörgen Jensen; Photographer Birgitte Urban.

CHAPTER 1

PLAYING IN THE ZONE

*"I want one moment in time,
when I'm more than I thought I could be…"*

From the song *One Moment in Time*,
produced for the 1988 Summer Olympics

"Ah, s——-, it's all happening again."

Roger Federer remembers the moment, the word, with painful clarity. "Again."

He was down 3-1 in the fifth set of the 2017 Australian Open final, losing to Rafael Nadal, his career kryptonite. Nadal, who was 6-0 against Federer in grand slams since 2008, pounded forehands at him. Federer felt his legs go heavy. Then heavier. He started talking to himself. "I recall saying, 'You have to try to break now, pal, because later on he is going to stay in the lead and have the break, and then too much luck is involved to turn the whole thing around.'"

More than any player in the modern era, Roger Federer has made the game look easy. Federer, the graceful. Federer, the perfect. Federer, the ideal tennis player. It's what makes him so intoxicating to watch. It's what inspires a near literal traveling church of Roger Federer faithful at ATP events. But what looks easy comes with a soundtrack, an internal monologue, and in that monologue, the greatest male tennis player of all time will sometimes grind hard, full of doubt and pressure and frustration, wrestling with history and ambition, fearful of coming up short.

"Oh, s——-, he's got me at the finish line," Federer said to himself.

MIND OVER TENNIS

He struggled to calm down. He kept talking, tried to stay positive: "I told myself, 'I've done very little wrong. I've played committed. I've played bigger with my backhand than I ever have against Rafa. I've hit a lot of backhand winners.'"

He was resetting, centering himself in the middle of a free fall. And somewhere in the conversation between Federer and Federer he found the calm he was seeking. This was an unlikely final to be in, coming off a left knee injury at age 35, and the boisterous crowd was with him. He fed on its energy. He remembers it now as some combination of Zen and excitement. "A different mindset," he says. Instead of getting shaky, he got energized. Instead of reproducing an old pattern, he found something new. "I had the best 20 minutes of my life, maybe, on the tennis court," he says. "I just zoned in and just went ..." He lifts his right hand and mimics a jet taking off. It climbs higher and higher, and then it flies away.

Federer is sitting at a long, lacquered table in a private dining room at the Four Seasons Hotel in downtown Seattle. He is tanned and wears a black Nike top and black Nike sweats. He sits up in his chair, unspooling the moment in Melbourne, excited at the memory of it. "What I was telling myself is 'Play free,'" he says. "'Don't feel like you're in a straitjacket. Feel like you have nothing to lose, maybe for one of the first times.'"

With Federer serving for the match, Nadal made one last charge, earning two break points and threatening to take back momentum. Federer kept talking to himself, urging himself on: "Just keep not thinking too much about the what-ifs ... the pressure, the moment. I know it's huge, we all know it's huge, but just try to shake it off. Don't freeze up. Fight, but don't try too hard and want it too much."

He looks out the hotel-room window toward Puget Sound. The sky is clear and blue. "Just like Switzerland," he says. Snow-covered mountains rise in the distance. The view is scarred by an unsightly gray power plant. He looks past it to the water and the white peaks.

"I let go," he says.

From an interview with Federer about the match by Kurt Streeter 05/30/17 in ESPN Magazine.

FEDERER'S WIN is even more remarkable when you consider the circumstances. Roger Federer, 35 years old, was by all standards facing an almost insurmountable obstacle. This was his first major tournament after having been off tennis for 6 months with a knee injury. He had not beaten Nadal in a Grand Slam since the 2007 Wimbledon final and had a 6-match losing streak against him. After being 3-1 down and serve break in the fifth set, the match should have been over, considering how strong Nadal usually is in five-setters. But by some sort of miracle Roger managed to turn the match around and win. What Federer describes *as "perhaps the best 20 minutes of my life, maybe, on the tennis court"* is a perfect example of what's often called *playing in the zone*, a state where one is performing at an unexpected high level. It is every tennis player's dream to be able to raise their game to this level whenever possible. We will explore it more deeply in this chapter.

In tennis, it is often said that what separates the truly great players from the rest is their ability to raise their performance to the highest level when it really matters – such as playing the important points well. But even if they succeed in raising their level a bit when they need to, reaching as high as playing in the zone is still something very rare and special. Even for a player as perfect and experienced as Roger Federer!

WHAT IS THE ZONE? Many books on the subject of mental tennis deal mostly with the negative emotions and reactions that tend to afflict tennis players and lower their performance. Considering how damaging such reactions can be, this is quite understandable. Choking ("rubber arm") when you are serving for the match can be almost as debilitating as a broken bone. Even small mental reactions, such as getting upset over an incorrect line call and being unable to let go of the incident, can completely turn a match around, and in fact you often see just that sort of thing happening. Sometimes the mental disturbance can be as minor as letting one's thoughts drift to the possibility of winning the match and what this could mean, which then leads to a loss of focus and losing the grip on the match.

Playing in the zone could be said to be the exact opposite mental phenomenon: a player experiences a heightened state of increased focus, sharpened perceptions, close-to-perfect playing and almost magically performing way above the normal level of play. Mental coaching, in my opinion, does not devote sufficient attention to such higher levels of performance. Furthermore, if those mental states are mentioned at all, a workable method for how to get there is hardly ever mentioned. By focusing attention on the negatives, mental coaching sometimes gets a bad reputation so that if a player gets help from a mental coach, or sports psychologist, it becomes synonymous with the idea that "something must be wrong mentally" with the player. As a consequence, most players never work systematically on improving their mental game.

This last point was brought home to me rather forcefully back in the late 1990s when I was at an ATP tournament in Miami. That year there were lots of long rain delays, so I took the opportunity to ask several of the players about the mental game and what their thoughts were about it. I managed to talk to most of the top 20 players in the world, and their answers were quite revealing. They all felt that at the top level in tennis the mental game was all-important. They said things like *"it's 90% of the game"* or *"The players can all hit all the shots. The difference in the results is in the mind."* Then I asked them *"So if it's 90% of the game, how much of your practice time do you spend on improving your mental abilities?"* The answers ranged from a blank stare to *"uuuh, I don't really do that."* I finally asked them what their thoughts were about mental coaching. They pretty much all felt that it was not for them, since you only needed it if "something was wrong with you," and they were not interested in *"digging into their childhood incidents,"* etc.

Granted, this was back in the 90s, and the attitude has changed a bit since then. Still, my viewpoint is that players would benefit enormously from working systematically on improving their mental abilities, providing, of course, that the methods were workable and that they did not stop after handling only the problem areas, but continued until higher states were achieved.

In tennis, playing at this extraordinary level I described above is usually called *"playing in the zone"*.

Playing in the zone is no small thing. It's not like you just happen to play a little better than usual. Those who have experienced it usually remember it vividly for months and years afterwards. And when trying to explain what happened they have a hard time finding words for it. It's almost like a supernatural event; a spiritual experience.

There has actually been a lot of research conducted into this field. The phenomenon is well known by athletes in all sports, and perhaps you yourself have been lucky enough to achieve it a few times in your career? It goes under several different names, for example PEAK PERFORMANCE, PEAK EXPERIENCE or FLOW.

There is a bit of variation in how people experience playing in the zone. Sometimes it is accompanied by strong feelings of pleasure, sometimes it's just about high-level performance. Here is a list of the most common descriptions of the state:

- Performing at a level far above normal
- Total focus. Often to such a point that awareness of surroundings almost disappears (noise from the audience or other distractions are not even heard)
- Time slows down
- The ball seems bigger ("the ball looked big like a basketball") and it's impossible to miss
- Stillness of the mind. The usual "chatter" stops. Players often say that thoughts stopped and instead they just "knew" everything
- Effortless
- Positive emotions
- Not worrying about the results. Just playing
- Being fully in the present. No hang-ups on the past and not drifting into thinking about the future

As I mentioned above, when working on developing one's mental game, it is important to realize that the goal is NOT to just get rid of mental difficulties, but to aim for the very top. In other words, the ultimate success in mental training would be to achieve the ability to turn on the state of playing in the zone at will and when needed.

The question is, of course, how do you do that? And is it even possible to reach this high? As difficult as this is in tennis, it might be an even greater challenge in some other sports. Consider, for instance, Olympic athletes. They have to time their peak to an exact event, which takes place only once every fourth year, and then only at a certain specific time. Difficult, to say the least!

But here is a perfect example showing that it is indeed possible, although exceedingly rare. It is the fantastic story of discus thrower Al Oerter. Possibly he is the all-time master of timing peak performance, managing to win the gold medal in no less than four consecutive Olympic Games, and in every one of them he, for various reasons, was not the favorite to win. And each time he came up with the winning throw when it mattered the most and when the pressure was the highest possible!

Oerter was born in 1936 in Queens, New York. His start in life hardly suggested one of the all-time greats of athletics as childhood high blood pressure kept him off the playgrounds and training tracks. That Oerter ever became a discus thrower was an accident and part of the legend around his career.

A teenaged sprinter at Sewanhaka High School on Long Island, he was running on a track when a discus skipped into his path. Oerter, then 15, picked it up and threw it back from where it came, except that he heaved it past the team-mate who had originally thrown it. Oerter's coach saw it and immediately made him change his events to discus. Five years later, he was an Olympic gold medalist.

Oerter was never favored to win an Olympics. Especially not his first, in 1956, when he was a 20-year-old at Kansas University and faced world record-holder Fortune Gordien, also of the US. But Oerter managed to break the Olympic record with his first-round 56.36 m throw, a lifetime best and better than all his rivals by more than 1.5 m. (The old master took it hard. Gordien went home and raised a son, Marcus, and trained him to be better than his father. Twenty-two years later, at the Pepsi Invitational at UCLA, he sent Marcus, then 23, out to throw against Al Oerter, then 43. Oerter beat him.)

A year after the 1956 Olympics, Oerter survived a near-fatal car accident. Discus throwers are catapults in human form. Their arms and spines endure terrific forces in each competitive effort. The accident damaged Oerter's frame and he threw inconsistently over the next three years.

At the 1960 Rome Games Edmund Piatkowski arrived as the world record holder. Oerter struggled with nervousness in the early rounds, and only in the fifth, penultimate, round did he manage to throw 59.18 m, winning the gold medal. This time by a margin of nearly 1.2 m.

When the 1964 Olympics took place in October in Tokyo, Oerter, the two-time reigning Olympic discus champion, was once again not the favorite. Not only was Danek the world record holder, but he had won an incredible 45 consecutive competitions. To make matters worse for Oerter he was forced to wear a neck brace because of what was described as a "chronic cervical disk injury." That injury was far from the extent of Oerter's physical problems that season though. About a week before the start of the Olympics, Oerter slipped and fell while practicing on a wet field. He tore the cartilage in his rib cage. As he told Bud Greenspan in *100 Greatest Moments in Olympic History,* "I was bleeding internally, I couldn't move, I couldn't sleep and I consumed bottles of aspirin to alleviate the pain. I went through ice treatments to minimize the bleeding and the doctors ordered me not to compete. But these are the Olympics and you die before you don't compete in the Olympics."

Oerter competed with his rib cage heavily taped and packed with ice, and not even three shots of Novocain could dull the pain. After four rounds (each competitor got six throws or rounds) Oerter was in third place—a remarkable enough achievement given the circumstances, but still more than 2 m short of Danek's best throw. Acknowledging he was in too much pain to try a sixth toss, Oerter decided to go for broke in the fifth round. His throw of sixty-one meters was a new Olympic record and nearly half a meter better than Danek's best toss. Oerter never saw the discus land. He was lying on the ground, doubled up in pain.

Oerter returned to the Olympics in 1968 at Mexico City, but teammate Jay Silvester was cast as the favorite. Many felt that Oerter, who was then 32, could not win the event because he had never thrown as far as Silvester did even on his average throws. At the Olympics, however, Oerter hurled another Olympic record throw of 64.78 meters on his third throw. His record held and he became the first track and field athlete to win gold medals in four consecutive Olympic Games.

The examples of Federer and Oerter give you an idea of just how important the mental factors are in sports. In tennis we see that certain players appear far superior to others. Nadal, Federer, Djokovic: between the three of them they have won almost every major title over the last few years. So how much better than others are they actually? One way of measuring it would be to look at the total percentage of points won over their whole careers. You would expect a superior player to win far more points than a lesser player, wouldn't you? So what percentage of points would you guess Federer has won over his whole career? Most people I ask (and this includes highly ranked players and coaches) answer around 60%-70% or maybe even more. The actual figure is much lower: 54%. Surprised? OK, how about some of the less illustrious players.? Take Michael Chang for instance: 53%. Feliciano Lopez: 50%. Marcos Baghdatis: 51%. The percentage total points won is remarkably similar for all these top players.

Clearly, one conclusion we can draw is that the better ranked players don't necessarily win a much higher percentage of points, but apparently they tend to win the **important** points, which then results in a higher game percentage won, and in turn more matches. The same principle applies not just at the top professional level but at every level in tennis. The number of points won in a match are usually very similar for both winner and loser. The difference is **which** points they win and when. In fact, sometimes you can even see a match where the loser won a higher number of total points, but still lost!

In the example of the 2017 Australian Open, Federer managed to reach a higher state of *playing in the zone* for some minutes, and this was enough to turn the match around and win. With Al Oerter it was even more remarkable. At a single point in time every fourth year, and in each case with just one single throw, he managed to pull off a peak performance despite all expectations to the contrary.

What would it mean to your tennis if you had the ability to produce a peak performance and play in the zone at will, and when you yourself had decided it was time to do so? What if you could raise your level when you played important points?

Now you may be asking yourself if it is even possible to get these things under control, and, if so, could you yourself achieve this? The fact that Al Oerter managed to control, and bring about, an exact moment when he peaked, not only once, but on four separate occasions shows that it is indeed possible for at least some people to control it. And, thinking logically, if one person can do it, why couldn't others as well? And why couldn't you?

Playing in the zone, or as it's also called PEAK PERFORMANCE, is a rare occurrence, that's for sure. Nevertheless, it happens often enough that there are literally thousands of documented stories of athletes having experienced it. And a large percentage of athletes have personally experienced it at least one or a few times in their careers. This, too, would tend to indicate that most people have the potential of getting there.

At the same time we know that (at least in the sport of tennis) most players do not practice their mental skills in a systematic and organized way. And if they do, it mostly deals with lower-level problems and does not address how to reach the top state of playing in the zone.

I'm sure your burning question right now is: *OK, so how do I get there? What do I have to do?*

It's actually quite simple. There are two specific drills in the book almost guaranteed to get you there within a few hours of doing them (chapters *Consistency Training* and *Concentration Drill*). Done correctly you will get into a state where you feel like you just can't miss, and you can hit the ball without any distracting thoughts. Your mind will feel calm, and the hitting will be effortless.

That being said, there is more to it. Ultimately, tennis is about winning. Being in the zone means that you are performing at your best mentally. But even though the drills are almost guaranteed to bring you into such a state, it can take a lot more for it to hold up in a match. The state itself can be easily disrupted by, for instance, such things as unwanted emotions (like nervousness or anger) or distractions in the environment. Because of this, other drills are necessary.

Furthermore, reaching your full potential in tennis requires many things of a mental character. It's not just about being mentally alert or in the zone in match situations. For instance, how to train most effectively, planning and strategy, preparation for matches etc. All of these things are greatly affected by mental factors, and we will cover them in first few chapters of the book. As much as you'd probably like to get into "zone work" right away, my suggestion is that you go through these first. They will give you the why and how of the drills and give you the needed understanding to get the most out of them. At the same time you will acquire a general foundation for achieving what I call MIND OVER TENNIS.

CHAPTER 2

THE IMPORTANCE OF PREPARATION AND KNOWLEDGE

"Winning is not a sometime thing; it's an all the time thing. You don't win once in a while; you don't do things right once in a while; you do them right all of the time. Winning is a habit. Unfortunately, so is losing."

Coach Vincent T. Lombardi

THE TITLE OF THE BOOK, *Mind over Tennis*, is based on the term *Mind over Matter* which in turn means that through the power of the mind one overcomes the challenges and obstacles of the physical world. It especially implies that despite hardship and adversity one persists and sees things through to reach whatever goal one has set. In other words, nothing breaks one's spirit, and despite whatever resistance and challenges are thrown in one's way, one is able to keep pushing forward with a positive attitude and a powerful drive and determination.

Tennis is, as we well know, an incredibly challenging sport. It is full of set-backs, hardship, sometimes disappointment and even pain. To succeed, one absolutely must have a mind that is able to "be over matter". The term often used to describe this in tennis is *mental toughness*.

Mind over matter, also implies that through the effective use of one's mind one has fully mastered whatever endeavor one is engaged in (tennis in our case).

When talking about mental toughness we tend to think of it as something that happens in matches, especially at critical points such as serving for the match or continuing to fight even though the opponent is ahead in the score. True enough. We definitely need to have this ability to win. But is this enough? Or do we need to do even more in order to truly reach our full potential?

To answer this question, we are going on a journey to the South Pole. No, don't worry, we are not going there literally... we are going to study the epic tale of two polar explorers, who competed against each other to become the first person ever to reach the South Pole.

Polar explorers are about as tough as people ever come, both mentally and physically. Just to give you a little idea, have you ever had to be outside in really cold weather? Not too pleasant, right? Now imagine being outside in −30 to −40 degrees Celsius every day, all day long, for three to five months straight! What's the longest walk you've gone for? How about 56 km a day? Or maybe "only" 28 km, but then—just to make sure you're not thought of as a wimp—putting on a harness and dragging a heavy (100 kg) sledge along through thick snow, across crevasses and up and down a glacier? Are you picky about what you eat? How about surviving on a diet of pemmican (animal fat mixed with ground meat) and—to add a little luxury—dogmeat from one of your dogs pulling the sledges earlier in the day, and later on slaughtered to provide food for the men (and the other dogs). Afraid of getting lost and being alone and abandoned? How about being in completely uncharted territory, 1285 km away from base camp, and with absolutely no means of communication to reach for help? Such was the lot of the polar explorers.

Yes, these were tough men indeed. Fiercely, even gruesomely, determined and willing to do everything and anything to reach their goal. Certainly, neither one of them was suffering

The Importance Of Preparation And Knowledge

from any shortage of mental strength or courage. Why, then, does one of them succeed and one of them end up failing—even dying—in the attempt? What made the difference, and what can we learn from this story?

The story begins in the early 1900's, the "Heroic Age of Antarctic Exploration". The South Pole represented one of the last unexplored areas on earth. Robert Falcon Scott hoped to claim the bottom of the world for England; Roald Amundsen wished to plant the Norwegian flag there on behalf of his countrymen. Scott had previously, in 1904, attempted to reach the pole but had not succeeded. Ernest Shackleton (another famous polar explorer) had also attempted it in 1909 and had come farther south than anyone before, but the pole remained unconquered. Amundsen, too, was an experienced explorer, mostly leading expeditions in the Arctic. He was determined and experienced, having learned how to survive and travel in polar conditions from Arctic indigenous peoples.

Scott had two goals. Reaching the South Pole was one; doing geographical research of the Arctic was the other. For Amundsen, reaching the South Pole was the one and only goal.

In late 1911 the two teams set out on their journey. Scott followed the same route Shackleton had used in 1909. Amundsen piloted a new route, which was 96 km shorter, but at the same time took a risk by going through uncharted and possibly unpassable territory.

Scott's team consisted of 16 men. They were to be gradually sent back as the expedition progressed, leaving only Scott and four others for the final stretch. Scott gave himself four different options for transportation: ponies, dogs, motor sledges (primitive snowmobiles), and man-hauling (explained more in detail later). The motor sledges—which hadn't been tested in Arctic-like conditions—quickly broke down. The ponies were ill-suited to the climate and the terrain—there's no naturally growing vegetation to feed them, they sweat through their hides, which creates sheets of ice on their bodies, and with heavy torsos and slender legs, they sink deep into the snow with every step. Thus, the ponies made slow and painful progress and had to all be put down. The dogs performed well, but Scott did not feel they were reliable or well-suited for the crevasse-pocked terrain he would be crossing, and he sent them back to camp once he had travelled halfway to the Pole. That left three-fourths of the journey—there and back—to be completed through man-hauling—getting into a harness and pulling 100 kilo sledges, step by step (sometimes on skis), through the snow and ice for more than 1600 km and a rise of 3000 m.

But to Amundsen's team, the advantages of using dogs as much as possible was clear. The wisdom in selecting dogs was confirmed to Amundsen during one of his previous expeditions, when he had stopped to learn as much about survival in Arctic conditions as possible from those who knew the landscape most intimately: the Inuit.

Dogs were low maintenance haulers—they could be fed a variety of foods (including each other), and they kept themselves warm by digging holes to crawl inside. They also made great companions—breaking up the morale-sapping monotony of trudging through freezing wind and bleak, faceless terrain with the same four other guys for 2400 km. They were strong and fast, scampering over the snow and taking the burden of hauling off the men. Scott often marched 9-10 hours a day, while Amundsen rarely went more than 5-6, and yet in that shorter amount of time, he would sometimes cover twice the distance Scott had. Finally, because dogs can travel in colder conditions, they can run both earlier and later in the summer season than ponies, allowing Amundsen to start for the pole two weeks before Scott—a huge advantage.

Food depots were paced at regular intervals for both expeditions. Some had been placed earlier in the year, and some were placed on the way out. Both teams also relied on slaughtering the animals they had brought. Scott was planning on slaughtering the ponies for food (although, as we saw above, they didn't last long enough to be of much use, neither for transport nor for food). Amundsen gradually slaughtered the dogs to feed both the men and the other dogs during the expedition. But even so, there were 11 of them still alive and helping with the hauling when they finally returned.

There is a lot to be said about the journey itself, but to make a long story short, on December 14, 1911, Amundsen's team arrived at the South Pole and successfully made their journey back to base camp by January 25, 1912, with no human casualties.

Scott's team arrived at the South Pole 34 days later, on January 17, 2012, only to bitterly disappointed, realize that Amundsen had gotten there first. By then the health of Scott's team had significantly deteriorated, and their condition continued to worsen rapidly. The short Antarctic summer was coming to an end and time was running out. As they travelled north, they were slowed by unexpected cold, blizzards and sand-like ice that made man-hauling grueling. Forced to reduce their daily rations, they began to starve. Exhausted and suffering from frostbite, they knew they might not make it. Evans died one month after reaching the pole, on February 17. Four weeks later Oates walked into a blizzard never to return. He suffered from painful frostbite and could not go on. He sacrificed himself to give his comrades a chance to survive. Scott wrote, "He said, 'I am just going outside and may be some time'... we have not seen him since". Then there were three.

Scott and the two others were running out of food and fuel and were in desperate need of supplies. If they were to make it back, they had to get to the next reserve, the large so-called "One Ton Depot", where they would find provisions and fuel. But the unusually cold temperatures and violent blizzards trapped them in their tent. They never made it and died sometime in March from cold, exhaustion and starvation, about 10 weeks after reaching the pole.

They were only 20 kilometers from the depot.

The story of the two polar expeditions has gained much attention and interest, especially from the viewpoint of analyzing the underlying reasons for Amundsen's success and Scott's failure. It may seem obvious that the main difference between them was the chosen mode of transportation. Further research, however, shows many other contributing factors. Here are a few of them:

Because the men could not carry all the supplies and food they'd need for a 2400 km journey on the sledges, depots were placed at intervals along the route before the actual expedition began. Amundsen had spent a year creating a depot-laying plan for the expedition, and still felt it had not been enough time. He laid out his depots with regularity, along each line of latitude, and packed them with ten times more food (including 42,000 biscuits) than Scott's. Scott created his depot-laying plan once he landed at McMurdo Sound (base camp) and gave his men just a week to divide up the supplies and calculate how much to place at each depot. While Scott and his men died partially from starvation, Amundsen's team actually gained weight on their return from the pole.

Perhaps Scott's greatest depot-laying mistake concerned the placement of "One Ton Depot." During the depot-laying march before the main expedition began, the farthest depot was supposed to be laid at the 80th parallel. But the men were tired and the ponies were floundering, and Scott decided to drop the remaining supplies (about 1100 kg of them) right where they were, 60 km miles short of the target. This decision would prove fateful. On their return from the pole, Scott and his hungry and exhausted men laid down to die just 20 km from One Ton Depot.

Amundsen used fur clothes while Scott used the traditional woolen and wind-proof clothing. Amundsen had learned about this clothing from the Inuits, and it proved much more efficient, keeping the men warm, while still allowing air circulation. Scott's men were often freezing.

Amundsen was very meticulous about the equipment and therefore created a workshop where they crafted two pairs of custom skis for each man (one pair for back-up), modified the skis' bindings to be more efficient, created better designed and lighter tents (Amundsen's tents could be put up with one pole; Scott's required five), lightened the sledges, and sewed their clothing and remade their boots four times until they fit

The Importance Of Preparation And Knowledge

perfectly and wouldn't chafe. Scott's men, on the other hand, did refine their equipment somewhat during the winter, but spent a good deal of the time writing letters, playing sports, and attending evening lectures given by each other.

There are many more examples of Amundsen's superior planning and attention to detail. Both men were definitely extremely tough and hardened with a fierce, unbendable, forward drive to achieve their goal. But Amundsen was more meticulous and smarter about his planning. He furthermore tapped into the skills (such as dog sledging, fur clothing and more) he had learned from the experts at Arctic survival—the Inuits, and used this superior knowledge to gain an advantage.

Ultimately the reason for Amundsen's success was that he applied his mind to the fullest ALL the time, not just during the actual journey, and as it says in the introductory quote to the chapter: winning is not a sometime thing; it is an all-the-time thing! He not only had a strong forward drive, he also put his mind fully to all the details needed for success. You could truly call this a perfect example of MIND OVER MATTER (in this case, the matter and challenge of reaching the South Pole).

What can we learn from this story, and how might it apply to tennis? At least three lessons emerge.

1. Mental toughness is a vital and required ingredient for success.
2. Mental toughness alone does not guarantee success. Mental smartness is also necessary.
3. Attention to details and applying one's mind intelligently and meticulously is necessary. Not just in actual competition, but in preparation and training as well.

In tennis, mental coaching often tends to take a rather limited view of the subject, focusing mainly on how to solve problems of the mind arising in critical situations and in matches in general. Understandably so, since this is when cracks in the mental armor become the most visible. But taking a cue from what happened with Robert Scott, we can see the weakness of such an approach. What if there was such a thing as *"mental coaching for polar expeditions"* and it mainly focused on what to do and how to act if one finds oneself at the South Pole, worn down, with insufficiently warm clothing and frostbite, having no means of transportation other than walking, without food and in a blizzard?

Needless to say, such an approach would be disastrous. Clearly, the process must start much earlier and take into account ALL factors affecting ultimate performance in trying to reach the pole. The same thing applies to tennis. To successfully reach MIND OVER TENNIS, we must look at ALL factors that affect performance, including–but not limited to—effective training methods, relationships with coaches, parents and support groups, strategy, and technique. All of the parts together make up the whole, and all contribute to effective match performance. Winning is, as we have said twice above, not a sometime thing; it is an all the time thing.

Here is what Amundsen himself said about attention to detail and planning:

> *"I may say that this is the greatest factor—the way in which the expedition is equipped—the way in which every difficulty is foreseen, and precautions taken for meeting or avoiding it. Victory awaits him who has everything in order — luck, people call it. Defeat is certain for him who has neglected to take the necessary precautions in time; this is called bad luck."* -Roald Amundsen

In my experience, I have found that many important factors tend to get neglected, or be dealt with in a sloppy, even "mindless" fashion. To give just a few examples of what I'm referring to: ineffective mindless practice sessions; unclear, unworkable goal-setting; parents who (with the best of intentions...) manage to interfere with progress; mental coaching which itself makes things worse (!); lack of attention to equipment; and many other things.

The Importance Of Preparation And Knowledge

By giving attention to these factors and bringing them under control BEFORE competing, one can greatly aid in the successful outcome, mental and otherwise, of the match. Mental coaching should leave no stone unturned in building a tennis player who truly has a MIND OVER TENNIS.

One final lesson we can earn from Amundsen's example: it's important to be open and willing to take in expertise and knowledge from those who have already solved the problems one is facing. This holds true for tennis as well, and my hope is that with this book I can share some such valuable knowledge, sparing the reader from having to "reinvent the wheel".

ORIGINAL PICTURE FROM SCOTT'S EXPEDITION. MANHAULING.

Preparations and knowledge are extremely important in tennis. "Mind over Tennis" starts way before matches and tournament play. The future success of a player is to a large degree determined by this. Peter Lundgren's coaching career provides many examples, which we will see in the next two chapters.

CHAPTER 3

BAPTISM BY FIRE

The Marcelo Rios story
Peter Lundgren

I WAS FRESH OFF THE TOUR. The manager at IMG calls: "we've got this talented young player ranked 23 in the world we'd like to see if you can be his coach. His name is Marcelo Rios. Can you meet up with him at Bolettieri's in Florida?"

Unsuspecting and naïve, with nothing else in particular planned, I head on down to Bradenton in the beginning of 1996. We meet up at the academy. He barely says hello. What I didn't know at the time was that he had gone through a number of coaches and that each one had lasted no more than around a week each before they in despair gave up on the project!

The training went reasonably well, although I noticed that he would never look at you when talking to him. It was hard to know whether he even heard you, or if he just chose to ignore whatever you said (which, I found out, could sometimes be the case).

For some reason he found me to be agreeable as a coach (out of the long line-up he had rejected, in some cases without even trying them out). After about a week together he asked (in his usual gloomy tone) if I could travel with him. I agreed, and off we went.

First destination was Philadelphia where he got knocked out in the second round. Then Memphis, where he reached the quarters. Next Scottsdale – finals; Indian Wells – semi-finals; Miami – round of 16; Monte Carlo – semi-finals; Hamburg

– semi-finals; Rome – semi-finals; Sankt Pölten Austria – won his first tournament and then Roland Garros, where he reached the quarters. Quite an impressive performance. I felt quite satisfied with the result, and thought to myself that despite his quirks and the difficulties coaching him, it was worth the effort considering the possible bright future. Although, I must add, the "difficulties" were of a type not usually encountered by coaches (and that is an understatement of quite some magnitude). To give just one example out of many (I chose this one because it is at least mentionable in polite company):

While in Paris for Roland Garros we stayed at a topfloor suite at Hotel Concorde Lafayette. I think it was around the 20th floor or so. One day I come into the room and find Marcelo sitting by the window with a bowl of fruit. Innocent enough, right? Except for one thing: HE WAS THROWING THE FRUITS OUT THE WINDOW AT THE PEOPLE ON THE STREET! Pears, apples, oranges, all hurled out the window at unsuspecting pedestrians. I rush toward him and grab the bowl asking, "what the hell are you doing???!!!!" He says "what?" as if nothing has happened. "Don't you realize that you can kill someone if they get hit with one of those fruits?" His answer: "I don't give a shit"

And such were the days being Marcelo Rios' coach. It was, as the title of the chapter suggests, a "Baptism by Fire".

After the French Open Marcelo said he needed a break. I said, "what about Wimbledon?" He replied, "Wimbledon is only for cows", and so it was. Marcelo took July off and I went back to Sweden.

In the end of July we met up in Stockholm to practice for a week or so and then via Båstad to Gstaad. By then Marcelo had hardly been practicing at all while gone, so getting some good training in order to get back in shape for the tournament in Gstaad was of the essence. But here the next problem with Marcelo made itself known. He had a tendency to get temperamental on court, both in matches and in training. When this happened he would "bounce" his racquet on the ground, which often had the unfortunate consequence that it would crack. He had only brought 6 racquets with him to Stockholm, and by the time we were heading for Gstaad he had not 3, or 2 or even one left. All the racquets were broken! So we arrive at the tournament with an empty racquet bag. We called and found out that over 20 racquets had actually been sent to Marcelo while he was on vacation in Chile. But he had chosen to only bring 6 with him!

A few days later the new racquets arrived. But by then it was so late they had to delay his first match all the way to Wednesday, and only the night before was he able to start any practicing. Needless to say, he lost early in the tournament.

Next tournament was Stuttgart. Again, he lost early. One interesting thing happened though: I discovered what made Marcelo happy. He was playing football with a tennis ball. Me and Marcelo against some Brazilians. Suddenly he was smiling and laughing like a child! Nothing like tennis, where he almost always was serious and sour, almost like a thundercloud around him.

After Stuttgart was Kitzbuhel. We were going via Munich. Rios by plane and me by train. We were supposed to meet up at the airport, but when I got there I couldn't find him. It turned out he had gone to the tournament without waiting for me, as agreed, and without telling anyone. So I was stuck waiting for several hours until someone at the tournament told me Marcelo had already arrived there.

This, for me, was the last straw. I stayed with him in Kitzbuhel, but at the very next tournament (Amsterdam) I ended my time with him. It's one thing to have quirks and to be difficult. But when you can't even have common respect and courtesy with your coach, then it's impossible to work together.

Perhaps I should have known better. Already at the tournament in Indian Wells I might have seen the writing on the wall. Marcelo was going out to celebrate one night. I insisted on going with him since I knew he and alcohol did not get along that well. Sure enough, when I caught up with him at the bar it turned out he had been behaving very badly with some females at the place, and a few very large and upset men came up to me wondering if I was Peter Lundgren, then proceeded to tell me I better get him out of there or else "we will take care of him ourselves".

Some time later after ending our collaboration I met Marcelo again. This time during a tournament in Rome. I can positively affirm that I was happy I no longer had any responsibility with regard to his behavior or activities! To make a long story short, let it suffice to say that he again had misbehaved in a bar, and it appears that on the way being driven home from it had shown a certain finger to the local police. They were not amused, and he ended up spending the night, not at the hotel, but at a rather less cozy place, so-to-speak.

It was not all doom and gloom though. Some good things came out of our work together. When we parted Marcelo had reached a ranking of 8 in the world, and apparently I had made an impression on the tennis world by enduring and staying with Marcelo for as long as I did. Proof of this came to me some time later when I was contacted by the Swiss tennis federation. They had heard of my work with Rios and wanted to know if I could possibly help them with a young, very talented, but erratic, emotionally volatile and problematic teenager. His name was Roger Federer.

MARCELO RIOS
Drawing by
Roberto Bizama

MARCELO RIOS FOREHAND

CHAPTER 4

RAISING GENIUS

Working with Roger Federer
Peter Lundgren

WHEN I WAS TOLD about the possibility of working with this "new young Swiss player with great talent but troublesome" I might have been forgiven if I had declined and run away as fast as I could, considering the rather troublesome period with Marcelo Rios I had just endured. Maybe I'm naïve, or maybe I'm a glutton for punishment, but instead of excusing myself I decided to throw caution to the wind and shortly thereafter reported for duty.

What a good choice that turned out to be! The reported similarities to Marcelo Rios were far off the mark. Sure, Federer had some issues to deal with, but as I quickly found out, here was a person of a completely different character. Likeable, friendly, polite, respectful and great to talk to. (In order to not completely denigrate Rios, I should take the opportunity here to mention that we later on ran into each other and he apologized for how he had behaved during our time together and told me he had "had a lot of things going on" – so at least he had some personal insight as to how he had been).

But back to Federer. What a joy it is to work with true talent. And what a blessing to have been part of the team around what many consider to be the greatest tennis player of all time.

When I started working with Roger he was only 17 and had not yet matured as a player. A diamond in the rough, and still in need of polishing, he had some major flaws that needed to get handled.

I often get questions about this time. What was Roger like back then? How did he differ from other players? How were his "flaws" taken care of? How did he practice? I will try to answer some of these as best as I can and try to paint a picture of what it was like to work with this truly remarkable human being.

From the very first time I observed him playing his precocious talent was clearly evident. Even back then there was something about the smoothness of his technique. Everything looked relaxed and effortless, yet somehow the ball came off his racquet with amazing speed, especially on the forehand side. It was as if his arm and hand were moving in slow motion until suddenly everything exploded with amazing quickness right at the moment of impact. His hands had the quickness of a foil fencer. This is something I also observed later on, when we played other sports. His quickness. The ability to get maximum power with minimal effort. His serve was also already a powerful weapon, and it, too, was hit with very little effort and remarkable precision.

Who had taught him technique? Prior to me coming on board his main coach from age 8 onward was Peter Carter. Peter was very good at teaching technique. Even so, there were about 10 other players we worked with who had also been taught by Peter and Roger was visibly several levels better than them. I think the difference was how quickly Roger learned. If he had done something a couple of times, he would immediately master it. He didn't need to practice things like patters or footwork. As soon as he was shown, he could do it. This ability to learn things quickly was something that set him apart. Anything he put his mind to, he would quickly get good at. Sometimes annoyingly so, like for instance the time we played golf for the first time. I had played before and thought I was pretty good. He was a newbie. So what does he do? Hit the ball over 300 yards on the first try! I got a good whooping. Like I said: annoying!

He did have a couple of holes in his technique though. Backhand was a bit weak—which other players would quickly take advantage of—and his volley was unstable. Part of the problem was his physique (more about this later). On the volley, the problem to a large extent was his grip. He tended to hold the racquet so far out that one or two of his fingers were not even on the handle.

So what were the main areas of development that Roger needed? Nowadays when we think about Roger we know him as a paragon of calmness and focus on the court. Never acting out negative emotions. Always polite. Never tanking and with utterly inexhaustible stamina. Back then, it was not at all so. You'd be hard pressed to believe we are talking about the same person.

When we first started training Roger would run out of energy after only about 45 minutes of practice. His physical strength and stamina were way below where they needed to be. In matches opponents would be aware of this, and although they might be blown off court by Roger 6-0 in the first set, they knew that if they managed to hang in there, he would often run out of energy and they could come back and beat him in the following sets (which happened too often). At this point, and in practice as well, Roger would get disappointed and irritated. He (yes, Roger Federer!) would throw his racquet or just plain quit. It might look as if he was tanking, but I realized that he had simply run out of gas.

To give the reader an idea of how bad this might get, here's a funny story. The tennis courts where we played had just been furbished with brand new backdrop high-quality curtains at the end of the courts. I was standing there admiring them and talking to Peter Carter. I asked him "who do you think will be the first one to make a hole in one by throwing a racquet". He answered, "I hope it never happens". Well wouldn't you know it…no more than 5 minutes later a racquet came flying like a helicopter wing through the air and tore a big hole in the backdrop curtain and crashed into the wall behind. Who was the perpetrator? You guessed it. None other than Roger Federer.

He got upset and took it out on the racquet with his usual power. The manager was not very happy and called Roger's parents. The curtain had to be paid for, and Roger (who was quite remorseful) ended up making amends by cleaning all the courts every morning at 8 o'clock for a week. To his credit Roger dutifully complied.

Let me talk a little bit about tennis parents. In my experience as a coach, I have found that they sometimes can be problematic or behave in a counter-productive way. Rogers parents were a perfect example of how tennis parents ideally should be, I think. They did not get involved in the actual training—they let the coaches do their job. But they were totally fulfilling their role as parents, supporting Roger and insisting that he behave well and treat others with respect. They were very cooperative in handling, for instance, the incident above. I think this stable support is an important part of why Roger became who he is today.

In practice he would, as I mentioned, run out of energy and start missing. It could even look like he was tanking. He would then just go for a winner and one out of three things would result: win the point, miss, or hit the ball out of the court altogether. I think he just wanted to end the point, regardless of the outcome. He could, at these times, also become quite temperamental and angry.

Since Roger's weaker backhand side and his lack of physical stamina were major problems in his development, we decided to add a physical coach to our team. Pierre Paganini was our choice, and he remained with Roger thereafter. Pierre had been coaching Marc Rosset, who had been making major progress under his guidance. With this addition, Roger started improving gradually and little by little we could increase his practice time from 45 minutes to 1 hour to finally about 2 hours at a time. Along with this, his backhand improved and opponents had more difficulty taking advantage of his left side. With physical improvement we also saw his mental approach get better (fewer outbursts, etc.).

There were still some improvements needed in the mental game though. One odd phenomenon that happened from time to time was that Roger would absolutely crush the opponent in the beginning of the match (like 6-0) and then suddenly start playing much worse. Hitting drop shots or other silly tricks at the wrong time. This caused the opponent to get back into the match, and only when it led to a crisis (like 5-6 against him) would Roger engage again and find a way out of the crisis. This continued for some time in his career, although to a much lesser extent. I would talk to him about this, and one day he told me the reason. "I get bored when I win so easily, so I make it interesting". Well, it got better with time, and these days he has developed great savvy and plays the percentages relentlessly.

Another funny oddity surfaced early on. In practice matches I noticed that Roger would constantly ask me what the score was. I was puzzled. What's going on? Can't the guy count? Why does he have to ask me all the time? It turned out the reason was that he was focusing so heavily on practicing something specific that he forgot all about the score. In fact, he didn't really care if he won or lost, he just wanted to figure out some specific skill or combination and try it out in play. I believe this helped him in making fast progress where others might have been more concerned about the score. In a long-term perspective I think other players can learn something from this.

I mentioned what a quick learner Roger was (and is). This extended to all kinds of sports (football, racquetball, badminton, ping-pong and more). But also to such things as videogames. He would get through a game in a couple of days that would take others weeks. Very intelligent. This was also evident in how he went about developing his tennis. His father would often video his matches, and Roger would study and analyze them in detail for hours. When he saw something he did wrong, he would correct it and it would not happen again. We would discuss his matches and he was (unlike a certain Mr. Rios) a very good listener. At the same time, you really had to be on your toes being a coach for Roger. He would put high demands on you and insist you did your best at all times. So for me, it helped my own development to work with him. I think holding the team around you accountable and demanding high standards in absolutely vital for success.

One question I often get asked is about Roger's mental game. What is it that makes him able to win tight matches? Why does he not choke or seem to get nervous at critical points in a match? In addition to his amazing physical skills, hand-eye coordination and fantastic movement, I think that the mental part of his game might be the number one reason for his outstanding results over the years.

Does he get nervous? Most definitely. Everyone does. But first of all he does not show it outwardly, even though he would often complain to me about "feeling tight". Secondly, somehow this feeling does not seem to impact his game. Nervous and tight? OK, let me serve an ace, seems to be the response. I have no good explanation for this skill. Probably something you're just born with. Possibly it has something to do with his superior technique and hand-eye coordination. When a player gets nervous, technique weaknesses tend to get more prominent, and hand-eye coordination worsens (mishitting balls you would normally have no problem with). In Roger's case it could be that he has so few holes in his technique and such great ball perception that lowering these factors slightly does not have a visible impact on his playing skills. Just a guess.

Another aspect of his mental game is his almost uncanny ability to find a way out of critical or seemingly impossible situations. I can't count the number of times I have witnessed Roger pushed to the very edge of losing, only to somehow come up with a solution and turn the match around. As a case in point, later on in my career I was coaching Stan Wawrinka in Stockholm Open. He was meeting Federer, who he had lost to innumerable times. I told him he had a chance, and he just needed to go out there and play his game, he had it in him to win against Federer. And out he went and just pummeled Federer. I think it was 6-1, 3-1. Again, I was sure Fed should lose. But just then, at the very last moment, Roger finds a little opening (maybe a missed serve or passing shot at a critical point) and suddenly he is in the match again. Wawrinka lost.

Roger is like a mouse that somehow finds a hole to escape into just as the cat is about to catch him. Again, I think this is something you are just born with. You can't teach it.

One problem he had earlier on was that he would get upset when he made mistakes or lost serve, for instance. He would tend to dwell on this and react with negative emotions/anger. It could get so bad that Peter Carter had to take him off court and tell him to just sit there for a while. He would accept this though. He knew what he was doing was not acceptable.

He gradually got better at mastering his emotions. At first he tried to just stop it all, but the result was that he lost energy and became too laid back. Then he learned to control and direct his emotions and to focus on the next point rather than what happened before. We talked a lot about this, but ultimately I think he figured it out on his own.

With Roger's mental skills improving as well as physical strength and stamina, his confidence grew and it started showing in his results. He won the Orange Bowl when he was still 17 (the 18-year-old category). Roger Federer's first tournament as a professional was the ATP Gstaad in 1998, where he faced Lucas Arnold Ker in the round of 32 and lost, 4–6, 4–6. Federer's first final came at the Marseille Open, which was in 2000, and he lost to fellow Swiss Marc Rosset, 6–2, 3–6, 6–7. Federer's real breakthrough and first tournament win was at the 2001 Milan Indoor tournament, where he defeated Julien Boutter, 6–4, 6–7, 6–4.

It might seem like a long runway from the 1998 win in Orange Bowl to the Milan tournament win in 2001. People would ask me why Roger wasn't winning more. He seemed so talented, what's the problem? I think the problem was exactly that: his talent. He had so many weapons and so many things he could do on a tennis court that it took some time to put it all together. I told people to just wait. It will take some time. But then it won't be so much fun for the other players, and he will keep doing it for a long time! It appears my prophecy was right.

In 2001 Federer had the one epic match where he beat Sampras in Wimbledon. Was Federer done with his early development at this point? I will tell you a funny story from around that time and you be the judge of his maturity...

At the tournament in Halle on June 11, 2001, Federer was to meet Patrick Rafter in the quarter finals. With the match starting in about an hour I was wondering where Roger was. He needed to warm up for the match, but he was nowhere to be found on any of the courts. The hotel was close to the tennis arena, so I called him in his room. Here is what transpired:

Peter: "Hey, you have match soon. You need to warm up."
RF: "I don't want to warm up."
Peter: "What do you mean??? You have a quarter final. You HAVE to warm up."
Roger: "Nope. Don't wanna. I don't care about warming up."
Peter: "Not OK. I'm coming up to your room right now!

So I went to his room and knocked on the door. Roger opened. Looked a bit disheveled and clothes were strewn around the room, quite a mess.

Peter: You need to warm up for the match.
Roger: "Only on one condition. You and I are going to fight and wrestle about it".
Peter:" WHAT????"
Roger: "That's right. We are going to wrestle about it."

At that he leaps at me and pulls me down on his bed. A wild wrestle match ensues. Roger is by now strong as an ox, and within a few minutes I'm totally exhausted. Roger lets go, and with a smile says "See, now I'm warmed up".

He lost the match. And this (believe it or not) is the very same Roger Federer who only two weeks after this incident beat Sampras in Wimbledon!

Federer was quite nervous before the match. So what can you as a coach do to help out? When you get to that level in tennis it's not so much about detailed instruction for this or that. It's more of a mental thing. I told Federer that he had a real chance of winning if he just played his game and let loose on the court. So he did. It turned out to be a tremendous and epic match. In many ways the turning over of the baton as the world number one. Federer won this match, but then lost to Henman in the next. He had proven himself as a tennis player though and at this point you could say he had found his game and how to use his skills. The diamond had been cut and polished. The flower of his genius had started blooming.

We stayed together as a team for a while longer, and I had the joy of being with him when he won his maiden Wimbledon title. A very happy moment, and I am surely grateful that I didn't say "no" when offered the chance to come and work with Roger.

ROGER FEDERER WITH PETER LUNDGREN. BACKHAND PRACTICE.

PART TWO

In the next few chapters we will cover the following topics:

- How to train most effectively
- How to analyze matches and training
- The importance of consistency and how to achieve it

CHAPTER 5

EFFECTIVE TRAINING: QUANTITY OR QUALITY?

The problem
WITH TENNIS evolving from its beginnings in England in the 1870s, to the open era, and finally to the vast enterprise we see today, the money in the sport has gradually increased and at the same time the game itself has become more and more competitive and more and more physical.

As a consequence, the players train harder and harder, and for longer and longer hours. Most players at the top level push their training to the limits of pain and injury, and sometimes beyond. To make things worse, tennis is one of the very few sports that has no real off-season. The end result is a rather untenable situation. Consider, for instance, how many of the top players recently have been out with injuries for prolonged time periods, even needing surgery. Just on the men's side, over the last few of years, we have seen Federer, Nadal, Djokovic, Murray, Wawrinka and Raonic take time off. Some with career-threatening, physical problems.

The obvious question is: what to do? How can a player reach, and stay, at the top level without damaging his body? Training less would not work since this would adversely affect performance (or so it's thought).

Against this problematic background we can clearly see the urgent and vital need for the most effective training methods possible. "Effective," in this context, would mean methods that produce positive gain in shorter time and with less strain and wear on the body.

In keeping with the lessons we learned from Amundsen in the last chapter, we need to be meticulous and intelligent in every aspect of our training and not be—as it were—mindless about what we do with the limited time we have available. After all, there is only so much training you can fit into a day, and that time needs to be spent wisely.

Let's start by taking a good look at what a training session or full training day usually looks like. Can we find any ineffectiveness? Any useless activities? Any activity too hard on the body for no good reason? Or, to put it more bluntly, any mindlessness or idiocy?

I make a habit of asking tennis players about their training – specifically questions like the ones above. I'm sad to say that their answer is often a dismayed "Yes. Lots of what we have to do in training are things I already know, and I don't feel I spend enough time on the things I really have difficulty with."

My own observation of hundreds of practice sessions is that they often look something like this:

1. Short warmup. Sometimes short balls from the service line, and then from the base line. About 5-10 minutes while coach watches.
2. Crosscourt hitting from the baseline. First forehand, then backhand. Maybe 20-30 minutes.
3. Simple baseline drills, such as crosscourt/down-the-line, alternating who hits cross and who hits down the line. Maybe 20 minutes or so. The coach watches and feeds balls as the players miss. Possibly a few comments are heard from the coach.
4. Various drills, usually around 15 minutes each. For instance one player at the net hitting volleys, the other at the baseline. The net player hits a volley in a predetermined direction. Then the baseliner tries to pass. Coach occasionally says a word or two, such as watch your footwork, or hit the volley more firmly. A few

different drills of this type are done, lasting perhaps 40 minutes.
5. Playing points from the baseline, first to 7. Not much input from the coach. 20 minutes or so of this.
6. Serve practice for 10 minutes. Maybe with returning, or else both players just serve. Occasionally cones are placed in the serve square for targets. Coach might say a word or two about service motion, but mostly lets the players just practice.
7. Possibly a tie break or two is played. 15-20 minutes.
8. If time allows, a whole set might be played. Coach might have a few comments afterward, but usually not during the set itself.

Some of these points might be cut a bit short or skipped to fit it all in. Total time on court 22.5 hours.

A second training session for the day might look similar, but more time spent playing points or a set or two. When points are played there is not much coach interference or feedback

Analysis

The steps above are of course just a brief outline, and perhaps a bit exaggerated, but I think it gives a fair picture of how practice sessions often tend to be structured.

Does any of this look familiar to you? And, if so, do you see anything wrong with it? Or is there nothing wrong with it?

To answer this question, and to be able to evaluate how good or bad the practice session is, we must first answer another question: what is the purpose of it? Why are these steps done in the first place?

If the purpose of the practice session is to get a couple of hours of exercise and burn some calories, then it's just fine. It will definitely accomplish the desired goal. If, on the other hand, the purpose is to actually improve one's tennis abilities then the workout falls far below par. Why does one spend time on a tennis court in the first place? Assuming that one wants to improve one's game and is serious about the sport (not just using it for exercise or entertainment), then there are about four different activities one would engage in: (1) warm-up, (2) maintaining skills one already has mastered, (3) improving one's abilities (technique, tactics, physical, mental), and finally (4) match play. Each one has its own purpose, and each one has its specific rules for how to get the most out of it. Let's examine each type of activity in more detail and see how well it might accomplish its stated purpose.

Warm-up. Although brief, this part of the workout is important. The purpose is not just to get the muscles going, but also focus and precision. This point was brought to my attention in an interview I once had with Jonas Björkman. He told me about a practice session with Stefan Edberg he had been allowed to have when he was young, and how it had taught him about focus and intensity from the very first second one steps on the court.

As they arrived on court Stefan attached weight straps to each of his ankles and proceeded to do 100 skips with a jump rope. Then they warmed up. After a while Stefan motioned Jonas to the net and with his usual soft demeanor looked at him and said "7 balls are on your side of the net. None are on mine." By Stefan's standards a virtual scolding... (To give you an idea of what a gentleman Stefan is, during his career he won the ATP sportsmanship award no less than 5 times, and after he retired, they re-named the award the "Stefan Edberg sportsmanship award"!) Björkman got the message, and ever since then made sure to be focused from the very first moment of walking on court. In our example of a practice session above I don't get into much detail of what's done in the warm-up, but often you see a rather sloppy approach, missing a lot of shots, not bothering with correct footwork or getting into position for the ball.

Maintaining skills already mastered. It is, of course, necessary to practice a bit on everything one knows, so that the skills stay fresh and don't deteriorate. The example workout above would be OK for this purpose, but it puts a lot of strain on the body without learning anything new. The same result could be accomplished in shorter time and more effectively.

Improving abilities. The vast majority of the time spent on a tennis court, other than match play, has the specific purpose of improving abilities (technical, physical, tactical, mental). This is where the practice session in the example falls seriously short, and for several reasons. Improving abilities effectively is a whole science in itself. To get the best and fastest results requires a thorough knowledge of how the body and mind respond to training and how to structure it optimally. In a later chapter I will get into this subject more in depth, but at this point I will just mention a few of the more obvious problems with the practice session, from a viewpoint of improving abilities (by no means a complete list).

The practice session above is a mix of various bits and pieces. It has no clear overall purpose and plan. Doing a little bit of each is not the most effective way of getting results. It is far better to pick one or two points, derived from a long-term plan, and to focus on these.

The players do drills of such a level of difficulty that there are lots of mistakes committed. The result is negative, in that the errors become part of the "program" that the body learns. A small number of errors are OK and needed, but if there are too many it destroys the positive effect of drilling.

When playing practice points, the coach hardly gives any input. The main purpose of practice points is to improve tactics and play patterns in general (such as shot selection). The way to learn from such drills is by frequent feedback and reflection over the points played.

Ten minutes of serve practice is far too little. Serve is the most important shot and needs regular and intensive attention until perfected.

Serve returning is almost entirely missing as a drill, although it is the second most important shot after the serve.

There are no exact measurements of progress, or a clear target set for the standards required in each drill. Having an exact, specific goal facilitates actually achieving it. The target of "get better" is not specific enough to motivate full involvement.

There is a lack of "benchmark." I don't describe this in the practice session steps, but we can easily assume that it is missing, since most coaches or academies lack this tool. With benchmark I mean having a comparison to the standard of the better players. What is the precision of a Federer serve? How fast does a Serena

Williams move? What is the speed and spin of Nadal's forehand? How a player rates on these parameters is rarely, if ever, measured. The only real measurement of progress used regularly is ranking, but ranking is not something you can directly control. What can be objectively known and measured is only how well you perform the various parts of the game.

Match play. The little bit of competing that was done during the practice session would not really qualify as proper match play, and even if it were, the time spent was too short.

So what is our conclusion? Was there anything wrong with the practice session? The answer is a most definite and emphatic YES. Especially in the area of improving abilities and match play.

One would assume that the main reason a tennis player spends time on a tennis court (other than match play) is to improve abilities, and this is where this type of practice is most seriously flawed. The result of the practice is overwork, slow progress overall, and much frustration.

Some players (and coaches) are completely unaware of the unworkability of this approach. Some players know they are not progressing as they would like to, but don't know what's wrong or what to do about it.

Quality or quantity?
The answer is that quality definitely comes first, and quantity is important too, but should be limited by two factors: first, staying within what the body can take without overstressing

it and second, limiting the quantity to a point where it still produces positive results in terms of improving abilities.

Do not spend time on court just "because you're supposed to" or because "more is always better".

CHAPTER 6

UNDERSTANDING THE PRINCIPLES OF TRAINING

An investment in knowledge pays the best interest.

Benjamin Franklin

THIS CHAPTER COVERS some of the most important knowledge for a tennis player to possess. With this knowledge the player can be less coach-dependent and is better able to take charge of his or her own destiny.

The principles of training aren't really that hard to grasp, yet most players (and, truth be said, many coaches as well) miss some of the key points. Of course, ANY practice, even if it isn't perfect, will be of some use. But as Vince Lombardi once famously said *"Practice does not make perfect. Only perfect practice makes perfect."*

The human body is truly remarkable. Imagine, as a comparison, that you take your car out for a drive. As an experiment you push it to the very limit, stepping on the brakes, burning rubber, taking curves too fast and skidding around. You try to get the car to go faster than it really can. You keep at it for a couple of hours, and then park it back in the garage. You then repeat doing the same thing every day for a couple of weeks.

After two weeks of this grueling treatment, you take the car for an inspection to see how much damage you have managed to inflict on it. But to your great surprise you realize that not only is the car OK, it has gotten better! It can reach a higher speed; the brakes are stronger; the burned tires have healed and formed a stronger protective layer. Totally unexpected and quite mysterious. How can something like this be possible?

Of course, for a car this isn't possible, but, amazingly, this is how your body works. It does the impossible. Tell it to do something it can't do, and if it gets your message clearly and loudly enough it will GROW, so that it is now able to do what it couldn't do before! This holds true for strength, speed, endurance, and even mental abilities. Any demand you put on the body it will ADAPT to, so that it gains the ability to do what you ask it to do.

This phenomenon is called *adaptive response* and is what makes training possible.

The first and basic principle of training is this:

Tell the body what you want it to be able to do. The body will respond by growing and adapting to the demand.

The body does not respond to regular language though. You can tell your biceps to grow as many times as you want to. Scream, plead or cry: it won't budge. It only responds to actual physical demands and efforts to do what is beyond its current ability. There are three factors that determine how well the body will "hear" the message and try to adapt.

FREQUENCY
DURATION
INTENSITY

How does this work? Let's take the example above, trying to make the biceps grow. *Frequency* means how often you push the biceps to lift a weight. If you only do it once a week for instance, very little will happen. The next point, *duration*, means that you keep at it for a certain time. The longer the time, the more impact. If you only try lifting for a couple of minutes, the body will not respond much. The third point, *intensity*, means how difficult the task is, i.e., how heavy is the weight you lift. If you lift, say, a pencil your biceps will not grow, even if you do it over and over all day long. Too low intensity.

How does this apply to tennis? What is it we are trying to make the body do in tennis? We can divide it into three general categories: (1) physical (strength, speed, endurance), (2) technique and (3) mental skills. Each category will improve through systematic training, and each one will respond according to the same three factors of frequency, duration and intensity.

Out of the three, physical training, in my opinion, is the category of training that has evolved the furthest and which usually produces predictable and good results. I will, therefore, not devote much time to it in this book. The third category, mental training, is, as we have covered earlier, a greatly missing ingredient in most players' training regime and most of the remainder of this book is about this topic. Category two, technique training, is the category that occupies the majority of a player's time on court (other than match play) and where a lot of time is wasted or where needless stress gets put on the body. Sometimes it is even so sloppily done that incorrect technique is learned, resulting in problems in matches or, worse, injury.

This chapter will mostly cover the principles of how to train *technique* effectively. Mental practice will be covered thoroughly later on.

Making a muscle grow is pretty straightforward, which is probably why physical training is the category of the three above where training works the best and produces good results (and indeed is quite an exact science nowadays). Technique training, on the other hand, is a whole different matter. For one, technique is programmed in the brain, and the brain is not visible like muscles are. The process takes place more or less out of sight. When we talk about technique, we often hear the term *muscle memory*. We are supposed to practice a certain technique until it is "committed to muscle memory". This terminology is not really correct. The memory of a certain pattern is not remembered by the muscles, but by the brain – even though it might feel like it's the muscle that remembers it. Technique is a pattern established according to very strict rules and limitations. It has to be so strongly grooved in that the body performs it automatically on demand and without the need for further thoughts.

To get an idea of how to best accomplish this, let's do a little thought experiment.

Imagine that you are trying to improve your handwriting. It looks a bit sloppy right now, and you want to learn how to write legibly, beautifully and, on top of it all, quickly. How would you go about it?

What would happen if you just wrote a large volume of texts every day, trying to improve your speed as you went? Would your handwriting improve? Probably not. In fact, chances are it would get worse. Handwriting is an exact pattern of letter shapes that gets programmed into your brain. Engaging in lots of writing does not improve on the pattern. In tennis, the equivalent question would be: would engaging in a large amount of hitting or play every day improve on your technique? Again, probably not. To make this point even more clear, let's make another (rather silly) thought experiment.

Imagine that you have been given the task of forming a pattern of a large circle in the middle of a grass field. The rules are that you must form the circle pattern by walking on the grass, wearing it down to the desired shape. Furthermore, you have to accomplish it as quickly as possible. How would you go about doing it? Following the principles of frequency, duration and intensity, you would walk in the circular path as often as possible, keep at it for as long as possible, and wear something heavy to make the most impact on the grass. There is one other important point to consider though, in addition to the three factors. *YOU WOULD NEED TO WALK ON THE EXACT RIGHT PATH ALL THE TIME.* The more you stepped out of bounds, the longer the process would take, and the less perfect the circle would be when it was finished.

Going back to the handwriting example, we can see that the reason the handwriting does not improve, despite a high level of frequency and duration, is that the pattern most of the time is out of bounds – like a person stepping all over the lawn, but never hitting the circle. So what is the right way of doing it? How do you go about improving your handwriting, or learning proper writing in the first place?

It turns out that this problem has actually been solved, and the solution is very applicable to how to learn tennis technique. In 1840 a person by the name of Platt Rogers Spencer, developed a type of handwriting called Spencerian Script. You will recognize it from, for example, the Coca Cola logo, which is written in this style. Along with the script he developed a course in how to learn it. Can you imagine mastering writing like that? Well, people did, and it became the standard writing style for business correspondence before the typewriter was introduced. How did he do it?

The script was divided into simple basic figures, such as ovals and lines. The students practiced on these figures—and these figures only—until they achieved complete proficiency and confidence in doing them. They started out at an extremely slow pace, so slow that the shape formed was perfect, exactly following the prescribed pattern. Then the pace was gradually increased, one step at a time. He used a metronome (a device for keeping pace in music) to increase the speed by almost imperceptibly small increments. Once the students had mastered the basic shapes with perfection, and were able to write them at high speed, they started forming whole letters. Then short words, then whole sentences – you get the idea. When they were finished with the course, they were able to write beautifully formed Spencerian script at good speed and with confidence. The same method of progressing is also the most workable when it comes to learning tennis technique.

Now let's put it all together and see how each principle we have discussed specifically applies to technique training.

Frequency. Let's say you are working on learning forehand. You would hit a forehand as often as possible. Seems easy enough, right? Actually there is a lot more to it. Working on forehand for best results means focusing only on that shot and not mixing with, for instance, backhand or volleys. If you do general baseline drilling perhaps only every other shot will be a forehand. But it does not end there. How many types of forehands are there really? Just to name a few: normal forehand in mid-range, high forehand, low forehand, inside-out forehand, forehand hit with heavy top spin, forehand hit flatter for speed, running forehand, slice forehand (for emergency shots), forehand drop shot, forehand hit on the rise...the list goes on. And every one of those forehands has a slightly different pattern, a slightly different groove. So for the most effective drilling you would focus on only one type of forehand at a time.

The problem with this is that the incoming ball (especially if you are practicing against another player rather than a coach feeding the ball or a ball machine) keeps coming at you at different heights and positions. Therefore, the solution is to keep strict control of the incoming feed so that the player only practices ONE type of forehand until that one is mastered. Then the next and the next and so forth, until all are mastered. Then, and only then, would it make sense to start mixing them up, just as Spencer's students did not start mixing up letters or writing words until each part and forming all the letters was fully mastered.

Duration. Drilling on many different things during a practice session, of course, cuts down the time one spends on each. No more than one or two skills should be worked on at a time. Furthermore, to really get into and develop one's skills it is not enough to spend just a couple of training sessions on each. ANY training needs a clear structured plan (this applies to all aspects—physical, technique as well as mental). Based on an overall evaluation of the progress of the player and the established long-term goal, the immediate targets to prioritize are worked out. This could be as above) to learn a better forehand. These targets are then worked on in every practice session until they have been achieved. How long should one keep working on one target? Normally around 3-4 weeks is about right. In that time definite progress can be made. Less does not really do the trick.

Intensity. Now here comes a really interesting point, and maybe for some players and coaches unexpected. Intensity when training technique is MENTAL. That's right: MENTAL. How well a player performs during a practice session is often judged, based on the misguided belief that intensity always is physical, by how hard he or she worked. How intensely he chased up every ball and how much effort he displayed. This criterion definitely holds true for PHYSICAL training, but not at all for technique training, which as we discussed already, constitutes the major part of almost every practice session. I suppose I better explain how this is. There are several reasons.

Technique is an inner process. When you learn a shot like (again) forehand, you learn how to hit it byhow it feels when you hit it right. You FEEL the right grip, you FEEL the right swing. As you get better, and by paying very close attention to what you're doing, you gradually learn to feel even minute differences between how it should be vs. being slightly off. A beginner might hardly feel the difference between an eastern grip and a semi-western. For a more experienced player these two things are like night and day. The word intelligence is sometimes defined as the ability to tell differences, and in that sense the player is gradually increasing his tennis technique intelligence. The coach looks at you from the outside and tells you what he sees. But from inside (where you are) it might look and feel totally differently. A good coach needs to be aware of this and should always ask for the player's view, directing the attention to the player's inner feelings. To give you an example of what I mean: a while back I was working with a player on improving his performance on a certain forehand drill. His success rate was only about 60%. I noticed that his swing was a bit S-shaped and seemed to be causing inconsistency. I pointed this out to him and he corrected it, resulting in a success rate of over 80%. I then asked him what he had changed and how it felt. He said, "I tightened my wrist a bit", something we had not even talked about. But that's how it felt to him, and it worked. So I told him to continue doing it.

Putting a lot of physical effort into technique practice can itself be damaging. When you apply heavy effort, very often what happens is that your muscles start working against each other. It feels like you are doing more, but in actual fact you are simply counteracting yourself! Sprinters are keenly aware of this. Have you ever looked at Usain Bolt before a race? Totally relaxed! What you learn in practice carries over to match play and keeps persisting. Eventually this can lead to injuries and wear your body down more than necessary. A good example of the opposite is Roger Federer. His technique looks totally relaxed and effortless, and he has had very few injuries during his long career. Correct technique feels relaxed. It should feel like the racquet is doing the work and you get power by simply timing correctly.

Here is a third point to show just how important the mental aspect is in technique practice. An experiment was done with basketball players practicing penalty shots (you can read about it in the excellent book *PEAK*, by Anders Ericsson). The study was conducted by Dr. Biasiotto at the University of Chicago. He split people into three groups and tested each group on how many free throws they could make. After this, he had the first group practice free throws every day for an hour. The second group just visualized themselves making free throws. The third group did nothing.

After 30 days, he tested them again.

The first group improved by 24%. The second group improved by 23% without touching a basketball!

The third group, as expected, did not improve.

Developing correct and perfect patterns. Following the example of Spencer and adapting it to tennis, technique practice should always follow this sequence: first FORM, then CONSISTENCY, and last POWER

Form means shaping the shot correctly. This is done with the easiest possible ball feed, or none at all. The reason is that difficult incoming balls tend to destroy form and would cause the player to "step out of the circle," so to speak. A lot of the correcting one hears coaches tell (or yell) to the player comes about because the player practices with too difficult of an incoming ball and this knocks out his form. It is as if someone is continually pushing the paper around for someone trying to learn Spencerian script. Better to progress gradually and keep the form. It is also a much quicker way to improve technique.

Power is the final ingredient. It should not be added by increasing effort but by better timing and better technique. With correct practice and coaching you will find that even though the shot is hit in a relaxed fashion, the power will tend to increase all by itself.

By applying these principles, you will have accomplished several desirable things. Your progress will be much faster. You will put much less strain on the body. And your technique will most probably be more sound.

So, lets summarize this into a few simple points. On the next page you will see 12 points outlining the principles of effective technique training. Learn them, understand them, use them!

THE PRINCIPLES OF EFFECTIVE TECHNIQUE TRAINING

1. Improving abilities is possible because the body grows as an adaptive response to demand.
2. The body's response is proportional to the strength of three factors: FREQUENCY, DURATION, INTENSITY.
3. In technique practice INTENSITY is mental.
4. Have an overall plan and pick only one or two main themes to work on.
5. Keep working on the same theme for 3-5 weeks.
6. Always work on correct FORM first; never practice on a shot that does not have correct form
7. Gradually increase the difficulty of the incoming ball. The difficulty should not be so hard that it disrupts form. A minimum of 60%-65% of the shots should be hit correctly to begin with when the drill is started. If it is lower, the drill is too difficult.
8. Keep drilling at a certain level of difficulty until 95% accuracy is attained. This is usually the level of perfection needed for a shot to hold up in actual competition.
9. 95% success rate is also the level at which mental stability and confidence starts to build.
10. Learning correct technique is a matter of learning the correct FEEL of a technique. The coach should always be aware of this and help the player explore his "inner world".
11. Correct technique should always feel relaxed and effortless, as if the racquet is doing the work.
12. Power is the last ingredient to add, but it comes after form and consistency. If all other steps are done correctly, power will tend to come by itself.

CHAPTER 7

STRUCTURE AND PLANNING

DO YOU HAVE WHAT IT TAKES?

Sometimes I talk to tennis players who, sadly, have decided to give up on their dreams of success. When I ask why, their answer is usually something like "I realized I didn't have what it takes". In some cases this might indeed be true. But more often than not I find, when analyzing the matter more deeply, that the problem was not that they didn't HAVE what it takes, but rather that they didn't DO what it takes.

What, you may ask, is it that they didn't do? And might I have the same problem? After all, you seldom see a truly ambitious tennis player goof off or not train really hard. In fact, I often ask active players who have the goal of one day becoming professionals if they think they are doing everything in their power to get there. The answer is usually yes. They may even add "if I trained any harder, I would probably injure myself".

Here is the problem: becoming successful in tennis (or any other sport for that matter) is, in many ways, simply a race against time. Given enough time and a steady rate of improvement anyone could sooner or later attain the very highest levels. Unfortunately such a luxury is not offered though. There is a limit to how much time one can spend practicing on a daily basis, and how many years one can still improve, since age sooner or later takes its toll.

Training hard is good and definitely necessary. But for every player who trains hard there are thousands of others training just as hard and with the same level of ambition and goals in mind. In order to achieve one's full potential it is absolutely necessary to train HARD, but also, and perhaps even more important, to train RIGHT. Training RIGHT means that one trains in such a way that every minute on court counts and the most effect is gotten out of practice time. This is precisely where players go wrong. The training is not effective, and sometimes even wrong or backwards.

Take a look at the diagram below.

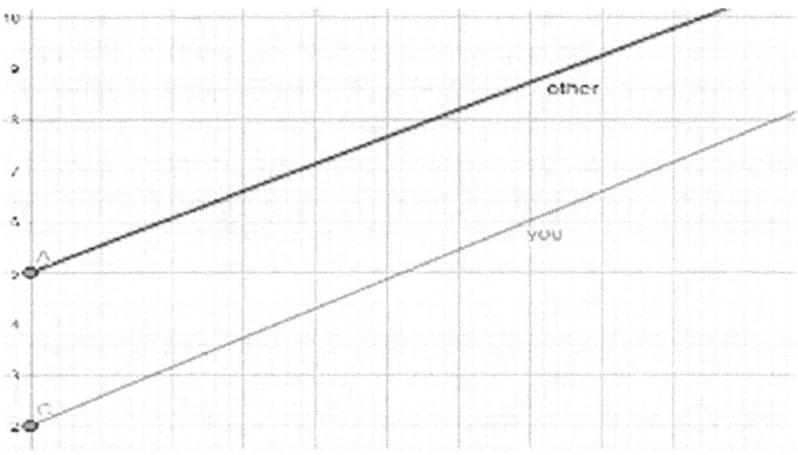

The top line represents other players, perhaps the very top players in the sport in your age group. They are steadily making progress. The lower (red) line represents you. You are also making steady progress and at the same rate of improvement. Now ask yourself this question: if I'm not the very top player right now, and the top players are making just as rapid progress as I am, then what is there to make me think I would eventually catch up?

Another way of asking the same question is: *how can I make my progress curve steeper so that I eventually catch up and pass those at the top?*

If you don't have a concrete and clear answer to that question, I am sorry to break it to you, but you are deceiving yourself if you think you will ever reach the top. I know, it sounds harsh. But if this is how your progress looks you will be better off if you get out of your delusion as soon as possible. Or even better, FIX THE PROBLEM!! It is very sad for a player to realize at age 25 or so that his or her dreams are not going to come true, and it is because of not doing everything it takes to get there. Then again, only a few players ever realize the true cause of failure, and instead convince themselves that they "didn't have what it takes".

We have previously talked about how to go about doing technique training. The chapter specifically covered the training itself, i.e., how to practice in the most effective way to get positive results. There is one prior process though, which needs to be thoroughly completed if the training is to lead to the best overall progress in a long-term perspective. It is necessary to accurately evaluate and determine WHAT should be practiced upon. What will make the most difference in a player's development? What are the strengths and weaknesses in the game?

Here is where some players (those who "didn't have it") tend to go wrong. Problems are overlooked, areas of development never isolated and found, basic faults are tolerated and not corrected. Practice is carried on as usual with the hope that the problems will somehow magically disappear.

Examples of this are sometimes quite blatant and surprising. Peter Lundgren once told me about a coaching session with Marat Safin. Peter wondered why he didn't use his volley more. After all he had both good reach and agility at the net. Safin confessed that he was worried about going to the net. Why? He quite frankly didn't know what to do at the net and where he should stand. Peter (surprised) said "Well, of course, you stand a little to the side you approached and basically cover the line." This was a complete revelation to Safin. "No one has ever told me that!" he said. And thereafter he dared go to the net and was quite successful at it.

It's problems like this that tend to never get spotted or remedied. Especially what would be considered "basics" in tennis, such as correct grip, basic footwork, basic ball placement and tactics, handling major mental problems and so forth.

Why?

There could be many reasons. Here is a list of the more common ones:

- Coach who does not really care. Just does what everyone else does or whatever he did when he learned tennis.
- Failure to recognize the proper sequence of learning, starting with and fully completing, the basics.
- Not recognizing weakness in consistency and thus failing to effectively remedy the problem (perhaps the most common reason for "not having what it takes").
- Player realizes what should be done, but coach says it's "my way or the highway" and the player gives in (maybe the second most common reason for failure).

So, what to do? Here is a suggestion for a few steps you could (should) take to get the overall strategy and planning right.

STEP 1

First of all you need to carefully analyze yourself as a player. In the business world this is what is known as a SWOT analysis. The letters (and what you analyze) stand for Strengths, Weaknesses, Opportunities and Threats. In other words, take a hard and very honest look at yourself as a player. Ask yourself questions such as

- What type of player will I eventually be?
- What strengths do I have in my game?
- What weaknesses do I have? (technique, physical, mental, match play)
- What has the highest priority to develop or improve in my game?
- What weaknesses do I have to remedy? (they might not be weaknesses now, but will become so in the future.

Like a weak second serve in the juniors may not be a big problem. But it takes years to develop and will be a definite problem as a pro, so better start working on it right away)
- What special opportunities do I have (for instance, exceptionally tall and therefore potentially strong serve)
- Are there any threats (for instance, a tendency to get injured in certain parts of the body)?

The list goes on. The main point here is to be brutally honest and to look not just at weaknesses (which some coaches tend to specialize in) but also strengths and potential future situations.

Based on this analysis you now develop an overall long-term strategy. Some things need to come first, others can wait. For instance if you have bad technique on certain shots, handling this comes before developing power.

STEP 2

Break down the long-term strategy into medium and short-term goals (sometimes called objectives). In the business world there is a useful tool called SMART goals, which helps in making sure the goals are actually achieved. The letters stand for **S**pecific, **M**easurable, **A**cceptable (or applicable), **R**ealistic and **T**ime-specific.

If, for example, the highest priority according to the SWOT analysis and strategy is to develop a better forehand, the SMART goals could look something like this:

EXAMPLE: FOREHAND DEVELOPMENT OBJECTIVES

- **Specific** objective. Develop a forehand with correct back swing, foot position, follow-through, spin, power. Make sure you have a clear picture of what you're after

- **Measurable** power of 125 km/h. Precision: over 95% lands within quarter court. Incoming ball (feed) also 125 km/h
- **Applicable.** Does this fit into the overall plan? The answer should be a definite "yes."
- **Realistic**. Is this achievable within the time period set and with the amount of daily practice time set aside?
- **Time**-specific. Objective to be attained within 6 weeks with minimum of 2 hrs. practice per day.

STEP 3

Structure the practice time. For most effectiveness at least half of the practice time each day should be devoted to this objective (around 1.5 to 2 hours daily). And a minimum of 3-5 weeks' focus on a certain objective is needed to really make progress.

Will the above steps ensure you achieve your goals? No, but they will make it more likely, and if you don't do them the chance
of getting there drastically decreases. Still, though, there is one more needed ingredient, and that is your own personal engagement and insistence. Once you know what you need to do and understand how to do it you must absolutely *insist* to do just that and never let anything or anyone stand in your way. Don't let external circumstances stop you, don't let coaches stop you, don't get tempted to cheat or skip on these steps, and above all remember it's *your* future that is at stake.

Finally, one word of advice. Since a player is always striving for higher ranking it can be very tempting to play as many tournaments as possible to accumulate lots of ranking points. Of course, playing competitively is part of the learning process, but it should not take over completely. Roughly speaking half of the time on the tennis court should be practice time and the other half competing. Neither one should take over completely. Your long-term development is the most important point. As time goes by and you reach higher levels you can gradually cut back somewhat on practice time, but don't do this too early. If, for instance, you aim for a professional career, then you should keep to the 50/50 ratio until you are at least top 100 in the world.

CHAPTER 8

A FIERY TIME WITH A FIERY PLAYER

Working with Marat Safin

Peter Lundgren
AUGUST 20, 2020, SAW AN ARTICLE published on the ATP website with the title "Marat Safin: The Man of Fire." I smiled. How very right they were!

We first met up in 2003 at the Lisbon tournament to discuss me becoming his coach. Marat had back on 20 November 2000 achieved the number 1 ranking in the world at the record-breaking age of only 20 years, 10 months (later to be beaten by Leyton Hewitt). But his ranking had since then gradually dropped, and when we met, he was down in the 70 – 80 range. He was seriously considering throwing in the towel and retiring. "Come on. You can't do that," I told him. "You are only 24 and you still have a whole career in front of you." "You would regret it the rest of your life if you quit now." So he reconsidered and asked me if I would coach him. I said yes, but on one condition. He wouldn't goof around or go for second best. If we were going to work together, he would put his heart and soul into it otherwise I wasn't interested. I wasn't going to be some sort of servant tossing balls to him. He smiled and agreed. I think he wasn't used to being talked to that way. Coaches of the top-ranked and most famous players sometimes tend to take on a subservient role. I, for one, don't have that in me, and I think it is very counter-productive for both the player and the coach.

We agreed to start out our collaboration at the tournament in Rome. I was going to take a plane from Gothenburg to Rome with a stop in Frankfurt on the way. Then meet up at the hotel and off to the tournament the next day. Little did I know how different from this plan reality turned out.

On the flight from Frankfurt I suddenly noticed a smell in the plane. It smelled like something burning. Sure enough, after a while we started seeing smoke in the cabin coming out of the cockpit. Of course we could not continue the flight, and the plane had to make an emergency landing at the nearest airport, which was Munich. We arrived late at night, but at least safe and sound.

The flight from Munich to Rome happily went without further incident. At the hotel I hoped for a good night's sleep after the nerve-wracking flight and delay. But no such luck. At around 5 o'clock in the morning I wake up. I think I'm smelling smoke. Again. Am I just re-living the events from the flight? Am I dreaming? No. I quickly realize it is for real. I open the door to double check. The lights are still on, but I am met with a wall of smoke in the corridor. There is obviously a fire somewhere. I throw myself on the phone to reception and yell "Fire, fire on the third floor!" All I get from the receptionist is "Calmo, calmo." So I repeat and continue yelling until it seems like he got it. By then I start hearing screams in the hallway and my room is starting to fill with smoke, so I go out on the balcony to be able to breathe.

Then I realize that Marat is sleeping in the room next door. He had the corner room, and I could see his balcony from mine. Apparently he hasn't heard anything or reacted since I don't see him outside. What to do? What can I do? I absolutely must wake him up, so I take a deep breath and go into my room to call him. At first he doesn't answer, but after a while he wakes up and picks up the phone. Desperately I tell him that there is a fire and that he has to get out on the balcony. Out there we discuss what to do. He suggests (like the wildman he is) that we should get some sheets and climb down. I tell him no way! It's too high up, and what if the sheets break? However, his room seems to be a bit better off with less smoke and I guess farther away from the fire. We decide that I will make my way into his room and we will wait there for help. So I dive into the hallway as quickly as I can and over to this room where he, with perfect timing, lets me in and slams the door shut.

We wait for 35-40 minutes until we finally hear sirens. Shortly thereafter the door is broken down and about 10 firemen order us to come with them. By then all the lights are out and there is at least half a meter of water in the corridor and smoke everywhere.

Eventually we make our way across the street, all black in our faces and coughing from all the smoke. We sit there waiting while the fire is extinguished. Other players are there as well: Haas, Mirnyi and others. All our belongings are left in the rooms. Clothes, equipment, etc.

Eventually the fire is brought under control, but there was a lot of damage. The hotel was a wooden structure, so we were lucky to get out alive. None of the tennis players were seriously injured, but 8 people died in the fire.

Somehow the tournament still took place as planned, and we eventually got reimbursed for our material losses (almost everything had been so damaged it had to be thrown away).

And thus started my work with "The Fiery" Marat Safin.

What was it like to work with Marat? By then I had been in the unique position of working with no less than 3 players who had all been ranked #1 in the world. It's interesting to compare them. While Rios and Federer had both been immensely interested in every aspect of tennis, watching videos when they weren't playing and so forth, Marat was the direct opposite. He wasn't really interested at all. In his time away from the tennis court he would spend his time reading heavy literature such as Dostoevsky or books on political history. One time Marat had an important match coming up next day. I asked him if he wasn't going to watch his opponent play. He said "no, you do it. I want to read." His political interest eventually bore fruit when Safin was elected to the Russian Parliament as a member of Vladimir Putin's United Russia Party in December 2011, representing the Nizhny Novgorod region.

I think all top players have a fiery temperament. I think it is a necessary ingredient in order to reach the very highest realms in tennis. Some learn to control their outbursts with time, like Borg and Federer. Others keep the drama going throughout their career, like McEnroe or Rios. One manifestation of temper is the racquet-breaking business. Both Rios and Federer had a tendency to break racquets (although Federer only did so in his younger years and then learned to control his emotions). Marat, however, was in a league of his own. His racquet-breaking was legendary. In fact, he is said to hold the dubious honor of having been the most prolific racquet smasher of all time, with an awe-inspiring record of 1055 total racquets broken.

This became a real problem for us when during a practice period in Barcelona Marat had suffered a number of losses (due to his injuries I should add) and in his rage had taken it out on his racquets. Three days before his next tournament we suddenly realized that he only had one intact racquet left! Now what are you going to do? I asked him. Well, we (that is to say I) got on the phone with his manager to order some more. He had some unmentionable chosen words to say about Marat's behavior and then told me he had no more. They had all been given to Marat already. How on earth had he managed to go through so many??? So the manager contacted the Head factory, but they told him it would take time. Racquets are tailormade for each player and they had none left in stock. The manager was in Tel Aviv, and the only solution he could think of was to collect some racquets that had previously been handed out as gifts to friends. Said and done. He managed to collect 4 racquets from various friends in Tel Aviv. Then put himself on a plane and flew them to Zurich where the next tournament was.

I guess this incident might have made some sort of impact on Marat. The next year I got praised by the Head manager for having managed to lower his racquet-breaking down to only 25 for the year compared to the usual 55.

Safin was, sadly, constantly plagued by injuries. As he himself put it "One year play, one year injury, one year play, one year injury." And so it went for his whole career. We can only guess what he might have achieved if he had remained healthy. With enough talent to rise to #1 in the world at only 20 years old, beating Sampras in the process, and with practically unlimited weapons and power along with a surprising physical mobility considering his size, who knows? The talent seems to have run in the family: his sister, Dinara, also reached world #1 ranking—the only brother/sister couple to ever have done so.

One reason why Marat was able to play at all despite his injuries was his astonishingly high tolerance for pain. I remember one time when his tendinitis in his knee was so bad he literally could not get out of the taxi we were in. Still, he kept playing matches. Another time, at Roland Garros, he had gotten blisters all over his hands. I don't know exactly why. Maybe his hands and the grip tape he was using didn't get along or something. In any case, his hands were literally covered with blisters all over. Open and bleeding! Having played professionally myself I know how painful even one blister can be. His were all over and ripped open/bleeding. This did not prevent him from playing though. Agonizing from the sidelines I witnessed him pushing through as if nothing was wrong.

Perhaps the most memorable moment I had with Marat was the 2005 Australian Open semi-final against Roger Federer. Roger was the overwhelming favorite to win. I don't think hardly anyone bet on Safin pulling it off. Before the match even he himself had severe doubts about being able to beat Roger. I disagreed. I knew that Marat was as good as anyone out there (or better) if he just let loose his abilities and played his game. I told him so. And I told him that I knew for a fact that Federer had as much respect for Marat as Marat had for him. Miraculously Marat pulled it off and proceeded to win in the final against Leyton Hewitt.

This to me illustrates how important it is for a coach to fully believe in the ability of his player to perform, even to a point of clearly seeing potential where the player does not himself. By seeing it and fully believing it, the confidence can transfer to the player and it can be made to come true. Without this belief all other efforts tend to fail.

In 2006, since Marat due to his injured knee could not play, I took on a job with British tennis. In December 2006 Marat called me and asked if I could be in Moscow for the DC finals where Russia was meeting Argentina. He had recovered a bit and was going to play for the team. He was a bit nervous since the Argentine team was very good (especially Nalbandian) and he felt it would be helpful if I was there. Davydenko won the first match, but Marat lost the second match to Nalbandian. Russia won the doubles. Davydenko then lost to Nalbandian so Marat had to play the last, deciding match against José Acasuso. Again, Marat said he was nervous after Davydenko's loss. I asked him "why? You are going to win the last match." And so he did. Pandemonium breaks out. Everyone cheering and happy. And then Boris Yeltsin comes onto the court congratulating them. Or should I say wobbles onto the court? I think more than a little bit of Vodka had been consumed while watching the match.

A fiery end to a fiery time you could say.

CHAPTER 9

MATCH ANALYSIS AND PLANNING

MOST PLAYERS have one of two conclusions when evaluating or trying to analyze a match they just played. Either "I played bad" or "I played good." The conclusion is arrived at through the simple process of comparing to one's own idea of how good or bad one actually should play or is capable of playing.

Not a very accurate or useful analysis. The error is further amplified by the emotions involved. Having lost a match often leads to feelings of anger, sadness, self-blame, shame and so forth. The estimation of one's playing quality is seen through the lens of such emotions, exaggerating how bad it might look. Conversely, having won the match, makes the estimation more positive than perhaps warranted, and tends to mask any errors.

Parents can sometimes be the worst examples in match analysis. Especially with younger players. If a match is lost the "analysis" involves pointing out as many errors as possible and generously sprinkling it with blame, anger, accusations or even (yes, it happens. I have seen it!) actual physical abuse. The purpose of this chapter is to look at how match analysis ought to be done. Certainly, blame and shame should never be part of it. Neither should exaggerated jubilation over a win. By all means, go ahead and celebrate the win. But analysis should be as level-headed and objective as possible to be of any use. Kipling's famous quote at the entrance to Wimbledon's center court definitely applies:

> *If you can meet with Triumph and Disaster*
> *And treat those two impostors just the same*

The main purpose of a match analysis is to use the conclusions for future planning. What areas of the game need to be improved? What seems to be working well and needs to be reinforced? What tactic works against such-and-such a player? Any errors that need to be remedied ASAP? Also, a match analysis can give some closure to a match, especially if the player lost.

In looking at a match, especially after a loss, it is important to distinguish between errors that were temporary for the day and more permanent areas of one's game that need to be worked on. I have sometimes seen parents sitting with a notebook, keeping track of every move of a child no older than perhaps 10 years, and then attempting to fix every mistake in practice the next day. The actual correct analysis would probably have been to just realize that this player still needs to learn all aspects of the game and to plan this out in a logical sequence. No further analysis needed really. "Why did you lose? Simple. You have not yet learned tennis and some others may be ahead of you still."

Ideally, an analysis of a player's game would cover more than just a single match. As we went over in a previous chapter (*"Do You Have What It Takes"*) we are interested in long-term trends of both strengths and weaknesses.

In any given match it is always possible to find numerous faults of various kinds. This is true at any level of the game. Even the best players will commit errors. These, however, should not necessarily become the subject of corrective actions or form the core of future planning. It takes thorough observation and judgement to correctly isolate those areas of the game that need work. The questions to ask are such things as: "What area of improvement would have most impact on the game?" Or "What weaknesses would be most important to eliminate?"

But even after arriving at a conclusion on the aspects above, it is not certain that this would be the first thing to work on in practice or that they would serve as the foundation for future plans.

The skills in tennis, just like in any other field of human endeavor, tend to follow a logical sequence of development. First things first. If we only build toward "winning the next match" we may miss out on the fundamentals—the basics. For instance, hit-ting the perfect backhand passing shot might have a great impact on match play. But logically, and as part of the natural sequence of development, the first thing to learn would be a correct normal backhand, hit with confidence. Mastering this shot will take time and effort, and meanwhile it might be best to ignore the passing shot as a skill.

In other words, with good match analysis we can find what areas of the game need to be improved and what works well. We can also see the outcome of previous practice, sort of a diagnosis. Do we need to work more on this shot, or does it hold up in matches now?

Look at a match as a diagnostic tool and use the results to help with future planning. But at the same time, make sure that planning is not exclusively based on match results. We still need to follow the natural and logical steps of progression in acquiring tennis skill. Fundamentals are always first.

A good match analysis will look into:

- How well did the various shots work?
- How well did the game plan work? (tactics, strategy)
- If something did not work, was it because the player really does not yet have that skill or was it temporary for the day?
- How did the mental part work?
- How well did the body hold up (conditioning, strength, etc.)?
- What might be the main reason/reasons for winning or losing? Was the other player simply better, or did some-thing work better/worse than usual? Did the loss occur

because of mental problems resulting in the physical skills getting lowered?

After compiling this information an analysis should be done for future planning. What, if any, of the points found would need to be included in future plans?

A good match analysis will result in a certainty as to what went right and wrong and what (if anything) should be done in the future to improve. A match analysis should be a learning experience. A match analysis should NEVER EVER be a time for blame, shame, anger or any other negative emotion. Even if the error or problem was mental the same rule applies (take notice parents!). It's just something to learn from and incorporate into future work, as needed.

CHAPTER 10

THE MASTER COACH AND THE ANGEL IN THE MARBLE

*"I never believed in myself before,
until I started to work with Peter Lundgren".*
Marat Safin

THIS CHAPTER IS ABOUT COACHING and what distinguishes the best coaches from mediocre or bad ones.

To succeed in tennis, it is necessary to be supported by a real crackerjack team. The most important person in that team is the coach. The mind of the coach and the mind of the player need to work in tandem creating a feedback loop: a true synergy, where the whole is greater than the sum of its parts.

To bring about this sort of powerful collaboration the coach needs to possess certain characteristics, and the player needs to be sufficiently aware of these that he or she can select a workable coaching partnership. What should you look for? And what should you look out for?

Good coaches come in all sizes and shapes, but the very best all have certain characteristics in common. What are they? This is where the subheading "The Angel in the Marble" comes in. You might wonder what on earth that has to do with tennis coaching. Well, the comparison is actually quite apt. Here is the explanation.

The Angel in the Marble

MICHELANGELO, perhaps history's greatest sculptor, was trying to bring into existence the *form beneath the stone block* in front of him. His own spiritual passion within him and his own desire to bring to life the beauty of marble were the driving forces of his talent. Two of his more famous quotes speak directly to it:

> *"Every block of stone has a statue inside it and it is the task of the sculptor to discover it."*
>
> *"I saw the angel in the marble and carved until I set him free."*
>
> Michelangelo

For Michelangelo, the idea was already there, inside the block of stone, whether by divine providence or his own imagination. His eyes and hands were merely the vessels by which that idea—the art—was brought forth into the physical world as he or God (or both) originally intended.

Here is one example of Michelangelo's sculptures. The masterpiece *David* created between 1501 and 1504. It is over 5 m tall, located in Florence, Italy.

The best tennis coaches and a great artist like Michelangelo have more characteristics in common than we might at first suspect.

In tennis, we are in essence building a sculpture: a future player, complete and (hopefully) perfect like David. A good coach will be able to visualize this. He will be able to see what the final player could look like. He will see the inner potential of his pupil, even before the player himself sees it. He will be able to communicate this vision to the player and make the player see it, too, or at least believe or hope for it. A genuine artist is not motivated by adulation from the public or self-aggrandizement. Neither is a good coach. Sometimes you will find coaches (or parents) who try to fulfil their own failed dreams through their players. They then tend to get very dominating or possessive about their charge and can thereby fail to act in the best interest of the player. One player I briefly tried to help, for instance, had the opportunity to come train with a higher ranked player (at a time when the Corona virus was rampant and good sparring was very difficult to find). His "regular" coach disliked this and let him know so in no uncertain terms. The result was that he had to go back to practicing with lesser players under the tutelage of the regular coach.

A good artist will, as we mentioned above, be able to visualize the final product from the very start. He will then adapt the methods and processes to best achieve the goal. It's the same way with a good coach. He will be able to see the potential of the player he is working with. Every player is different, and they all need slightly different approaches. Bad coaches will just go on routine, doing the same drills for everyone, or even worse, work under the principle "it's my way or the highway". Here is an example I witnessed. A girl I was doing some mental coaching with complained that her coach did not let her practice serve sufficiently—10 minutes now and then at the most. She felt that her serve had been getting worse during the time she had worked with this coach (and previously her serve had been her trump card, her best weapon). She pleaded with the coach but to no avail. He "knew best" and demanded she do the drills he had decided on with the argument that "I am the coach; you do what I say".

A good artist, finally, feels a strong passion and a deep involvement with his work and the final product. He doesn't just go about a daily routine such as perhaps a regular housepainter might. Have you seen the film *Happy Gilmore* (if not, you should. It's very funny)? The golf coach in the movie is a perfect example of what we're talking about here. In one scene he is sitting at the driving range on a chair next to a woman hitting balls out of a bucket. Reading a magazine, and barely even looking at his pupil, he occasionally says things like "good, turn the hips like that" or "watch the ball". He is clearly not engaged at all. Some tennis coaches can be like that, too. They just stand there. Go through the same drill in the same sequence they follow every day. Peter Lundgren told me about a coach he encountered back when he was training Federer. He had an academic education in tennis coaching and followed his teachings to a T every day. Monday was forehand. Tuesday backhand, Wednesday serve and so forth. Always the same routine, regardless of what player he was coaching.

I have had the good fortune of working next to several of the very best coaches in the world. Peter Lundgren, for one, and Magnus Norman being another example. I have always been interested in finding out what it is about them. What is it that makes them so special? The funny thing is that when I ask them they actually don't know! I think sometimes it is like that. The things you are the very best at—the areas of life where you are truly a master—seem so natural to you that you don't even notice or think that it's anything special. When I first met Peter Lundgren I asked him just that. What is it that's so good about you? How is it that you have coached such immensely difficult players and at least three of them achieved a world number 1 ranking? Peter thought for a while. Then said that probably others should answer that question. Then after a bit of further thinking said "maybe I'm pretty good with people" in a sort of doubtful voice.

"Pretty good with people." Are you kidding me? But no, he wasn't. With all his success and with his ability to deal with and turn around even the most difficult cases this is all he knew about it. So I had to observe for myself. What I found was that Peter, and other master coaches, possessed what I would call a therapeutic personality for lack of a better word. Not that they are therapists—they're not. It's that in the presence of such a person you feel good. It's like therapy just to be around them. Working within the school system I have seen similar traits where some teachers just "have it". With their mere presence the kids do better. They feel seen (or heard) and understood. They feel trust. They feel that they can safely communicate with the teacher. They know that the teacher has no ulterior motive. They just genuinely care about the kids and want the best for them. They can see the inner potential of the children, even when the children themselves do not believe it. And they can make them live up to that potential. Often when you hear interviews with very successful people they will mention just such a person. A teacher or a mentor that they felt "saw" them and believed in them. This made all the difference in their lives.

This is what a great coach is. A creator of people. A catalyst for achievement. Someone with the ability to draw out the best from their pupils. This is the inner essence of a good coach.

The seeing has to be completely honest and truthful though. Lip service doesn't cut it and is quite ineffective. We have seen several examples throughout the book of how, for instance, Peter's vision helped his players win. In some cases the player himself did not believe he could win. But Peter saw that they truly could. Then he managed to make the player as well see it. Confidence ensued and the player played his very best.

The genuine care factor is very evident in the best coaches. For example, Magnus Norman. Here is what he (and his player Wawrinka) had to say about their coach/player relationship (from an interview with Magnus a couple of years back.

> *Wawrinka: "He's been a great coach, friend and mentor and will always be a dear friend. I want to publicly thank him for all his hard work, dedication and commitment in making me a better player over the years. Winning three Grand Slams has been a life-changing experience for me and I could not have done that without him!"*
>
> *Norman: "One of the things he mentioned is I made him a winner... everybody saw before he could play great*

tennis," Norman said. "He told me that the words I'm telling him before a match calms him down a little bit and makes him believe that he could win in big moments."

I have asked some of the players Norman has coached. They all say the same thing. You just somehow feel confident when you're in his presence.

What I wrote above I believe is the rock bottom essence of a good coach. I don't know if this is something you can learn. Maybe you're just born with it. But it's certainly something you should look for when trying to find a coach.

This is not where the requirements for a good coach end though. He needs to have a thorough understanding of tennis technique, tactics, physical aspects and more. One question is: do you need to be or have been a good tennis player to be a good coach? Of course it is helpful if the coach has first-hand knowledge of what it's like to have "been there". If the coach is also a good teacher, that is the best. But just because you have been a good player does not necessarily mean that you are a good teacher. The two things are actually totally different disciplines. In an interview with me, Stefan Edberg had this to say:

> Now that I'm coaching [Federer] I realize just how complicated tennis is! Teaching is not at all the same thing as playing. Now I really have to think about it. Before I just went out and played. I think that coaching has changed in Sweden from before, when I learned. Back then the teachers were mostly pedagogues, teachers in school part time and tennis coaches the rest of the time (just because they loved doing it). They were all trained in teaching primarily and tennis secondarily. I think that's important, and probably the earlier situation was better.

We talked about the importance of understanding and empathy. Yes, they are the foundation and essence of a good coach (or teacher). Let this not be misunderstood though. It does not mean that a good coach should be meek or submissive to the player. Respect should always be maintained. Furthermore, learning tennis requires hard work and the student has to undergo much suffering in the process. It is important that the coach is able to motivate and drive the student to get through even unpleasant moments in his training or matches. Here is a good example of this that Peter told me about.

> *Peter: I was in Båstad with Grigor Dimitrov, who I was coaching at the time. He had morning practice with Robin Söderling one day. Magnus Norman was with Robin as his coach. Now Dimitrov is always super energetic and intense at practice and he was very happy to get to practice against Robin that day. For some reason Robin was not quite "on" and definitely not as intense as Dimitrov. Grigor was a bit disappointed as he walked off court. Then I overheard Norman immediately confront Robin. "What the heck are you doing? You just wasted Dimitrov's practice time. Not OK. Don't ever let me see such a thing again." Robin's shoulders sloped a bit as he left. I was somewhat surprised and a while later asked Norman about it. "Is Robin OK?" I asked. "Oh yes," said Norman. "He took it well and he understood. You have to set the limits for what is OK and what is not." Robin went on to win the tournament.*

Another example comes from the Netflix documentary *The Playbook*, where tennis coach Mouratoglou talks about working with Serena Williams. In the beginning of their collaboration Serena had been a bit haughty with him. Did not say "good morning" and was late for practice. Mouratoglou immediately put his foot down and told her how things were going to be. After that respect was restored and their collaboration proceeded without friction.

So being nice and understanding is essential. But there are times when "being nice" is not nice at all. The good coach has to make sure to steer the car back on the road if it's heading for the ditch.

In addition to all the above, the coach needs to have a deep understanding of how to properly analyze the player's game, how to practice most effectively, and preferably have a thorough understanding of the mental game. These skills can mostly be learned (for instance, by reading and understanding this book).

To sum it up, here is what to look for and what to look out for when selecting a coach.

- With a good coach you should feel "seen" and understood.
- A good coach should make you feel more confident and should be able to strengthen your belief in yourself.
- A good coach is there for you and to create the best possible you. Not any other motive.
- A good coach should be deeply engaged and passionate about his task.
- A good coach should not be afraid to point out when you do something wrong, especially something wrong from a moral or ethical perspective. When you fail at something, but honestly have tried, the correction should always be constructive not critical or demeaning.
- A good coach should be able to clearly visualize the future tennis player you can become.
- A good coach should feel respect for the player and should himself command respect.
- A good coach should have a firm and thorough knowledge of all aspects of the game, preferably also the mental game
- A good coach should be a good pedagogue and skilled at teaching in a clear, structured and understandable manner.
- A good coach should always have a clear plan for what is being done and this plan should fit in with long-term goals and ambitions.

I hope you can find such a coach. They are rare. And the true masters are even rarer.

CHAPTER 11

THE IMPORTANCE OF CONSISTENCY

When talking about a tennis player's skill level the discussion often focuses on how well-formed the shots are and how much power the player has. These things are immediately visible and perhaps this is the reason they get most of the attention. Meanwhile there is another factor that is at least as important, but that gets much less attention: CONSISTENCY.

Power and consistency BOTH need to be taken into account when evaluating a player's skill level. We could even go so far as to say that a player's level (how good he or she is) can be roughly defined as that power level at which the player is consistent. There are slight variations of course. The typical "power player" (like for instance Istner) might be slightly deficient in consistency, while the type of player who relies heavily on consistency (like for instance Ferrer) might have a bit less power. The point is that both factors matter, and one can not reach the highest levels in tennis without having a good portion of both. We can most clearly see this in the very top players such as Djokovic, Federer and Nadal. Federer is your typical power player, but at the same time has a fantastic level of consistency. Djokovic leans toward the consistent type of player (we hardly ever see him miss a shot), but at the same time has a good amount of power. Nadal is fundamentally a consistency player, but also has a fantastic power level.

If we take a look at the different categories of tennis players, we can observe how these factors manifest. On the ATP Challenger tour, for instance, most of the players have very well-formed shots and can hit all of them with good power. Where they fall short compared to the players on the main ATP tour is in the area of consistency. Sure, they can hit a powerful forehand, but how many powerful forehands in a row can they hit? How does this compare to, say, Nadal? How about if we compare the ATP players with the WTA players? What is the difference? Mainly power. Many of the WTA players are just as consistent as the men, but lack the power.

Understanding these two factors we can shed a light on some of the typical difficulties players have rising in the ranks. At the juniors level, consistency tends to be the overshadowing factor. If you can move well on the court and never miss, then you will be practically unbeatable since the power level is insufficient to hit a winner. Then, when the same person moves on in his or her career, the power level is suddenly not high enough to create an impact on the opponent on the challenger or ATP level. Conversely, if a player has a very high power level already in the juniors, he or she might be able to overpower opponents (despite their consistency) because they are unable to maintain their steadiness when faced with such power. But when this power player reaches a higher level the opponents are used to facing such power and do not miss. Suddenly power alone is not enough to maintain a winning record.

Perhaps at this point we should clarify what we mean by consistency. The word refers to two different (but related) features. First, consistency means that the player has the ability to hit many good shots in a row without missing. Second, that the player maintains a steady high level from match to match and also within each math. The dips (and dips are inevitable no matter how consistent a player might be) are never very low. In other words, their lowest level of play is not much below the normal or highest level. With power players the opposite tends to be the case: if they have a bad day it can be *extremely* bad.

We should also define what we mean by power level in this context. Power comes two ways: incoming and outgoing. Both are included in the concept. The power level of a player can be roughly defined as an average of those two aspects. A typical consistency player might be able to handle more incoming power than he or she is able to produce (again David Ferrer is a good example of this type of player). A power player is the opposite. A good example would be Karlovic, who can produce incredible power, but has less ability (for various reasons, speed of movement being one) to handle high incoming power. Again, with the very top players, we see that they have mastered high power, both incoming and outgoing.

As I mentioned in the beginning of this chapter, we often tend to focus on, and be awestruck by, the fantastic power the top players possess. So much so, that we fail to fully appreciate their equally incredible level of consistency in hitting these shots. This bias, unfortunately, tends to also affect how training is conducted. The young aspiring player (and coach alike) put most of their attention on developing good-looking, powerful, shots, while neglecting to fully monitor the level of consistency. Both coach and player may feel satisfied when a good-looking forehand has been developed and the player is able to execute, say, 15 out of 20 shots to satisfaction with no mistakes. This, as we shall soon cover more in depth, is nowhere near enough. To make things even worse, the incoming ball that the player works with is often a feed out of a basket by the coach. This feed has a far lower power level than the usual incoming shot in a match. So in essence the player has now mastered (not even to perfection though) hitting outgoing shots at a high power level, while at the same time not having practiced at all producing such shots against a similar level of incoming power.

How consistent is consistent, you may ask. Some interesting posts written by a person named Juan José can be found on *The Changeover* website. He came up with a way of calculating what he calls the consistency rating or efficiency rating, and he has posted actual stats from several matches featuring top players. Here is a link for more details of these:
http://www.changeovertennis.com/category/stats/consistency-ratings/

To understand the concept, start reading the earliest post on the website, which introduces it and how it's calculated. Basically he counted the total number of forehands or backhands hit during a set or match. Then obtained a figure of how many unforced errors the player had committed during the same period. Finally he divided the total number of shots that went in by the total number of shots hit, and then converted to a percentage figure. For example, if the percentage was 90% then nine out of ten shots went in or, putting it differently, only one out of ten were unforced errors. Mind you, this is in match play at full speed. Serve returns were not counted as part of this statistic though. Now, without looking at the figures below, what would you guess the percentages would be for these players? Again, keeping in mind that this is match play with the balls hit at full power, both incoming and outgoing, and of course purposely placed in difficult positions on the court.

Here are some statistics from actual matches:

Federer vs. Florian Mayer. Result Federer wins 7-6 (4), 3-6, 7-5
Efficiency ratings by set, Federer:
　　set 1,　　91%,
　　set 2　　84,5%,
　　set 3　　91%.
We can see that when Federer drops below 90% he loses the set.

Federer vs. Nishikori. Result Federer loses 6-4, 1-6, 6-2
Efficiency by set, Federer:
　　Set 1　　86%
　　Set 2　　95%
　　Set 3　　82%
Here the effect is even more obvious. The score clearly reflects the level of efficiency (=consistency)

The Importance Of Consistency

Ferrer vs. Nishikori. Result, Ferrer wins 6-4, 6-2
Efficiency by set, Ferrer (broken down into forehand and backhand)
    Set 1   FH 95%, BH 92%
    Set 2   FH 96%, BH 97,8%
Again, the result correlates with the efficiency.

What conclusions can we draw? Obviously even a small change in percentages can make a big difference in results. With Federer, for instance, it appears that as soon as his consistency drops below 90% he loses. What's also amazing is the high level of consistency these players manage to maintain in a match situation. Consider, for instance, the astonishingly high percentage of Ferrer's backhand during his match with Nishikori: 97,8%.

To get a better idea of what these figures mean and how they apply to match tactics, let's do a little math. To start with, we can easily recognize that anything you do in a match where you fail more than 50% of the time is a losing tactic. To take a simple case in point, if you like going to the net, but your volley fails in more than half of the attempts, then this is not a winning tactic. With groundstrokes the math is a bit different. You usually hit several in a row. The question then becomes how many in a row can you (on average) hit before you miss. This we can easily calculate mathematically. If, for example, you only successfully hit 60% of your backhand slice without making an unforced error, then whenever you are forced to hit two in a row your chance of succeeding is only 36%. You lose. If the opponent knows this, he would be smart to make you hit lots of sliced backhands. It's often said that you should "play the percentages", which is to say be aware of probabilities and statistics. You don't use low-probability tactics if you want to win. So it's goes without saying that a keen grasp of statistics is mandatory if you want to know what your best tactics should be.

What do the efficiency figures above actually mean? How good is 90%? And what does it mean in terms of how many shots in a row the person can successfully sustain without missing? Here is a table:

Consistency level %	How many shots in a rally can the player on an average sustain?	How many balls out of 20 are hit without error
97.5	27 (Ferrer backhand!)	19.5 (39 of 40)
95	13	19
90	6	18
85	4	17
80	3	16

We can now easily see why a small change in consistency can make such a huge difference in results, and why it is that when Federer drops below 90% he starts losing. At 95% the player can on average win any rally where he hits up to 13 shots. Already at 85% that figure drops down to only 4 shots. And at the unimaginable level of 97.5% the player basically never misses! From 95% to 97.5% the length of rally doubles.

All these statistics should provide ample evidence for why acquiring a high level of consistency is so important, and also just how high it really needs to go before it is of any major use. When you look at the level of consistency of the top professionals you realize just how high the bar is.

Players in general tend to be quite unaware of their actual consistency level. Often they overestimate. You yourself might be surprised if you actually try to measure it. One simple way of doing this, to get a rough estimate, is to hit crosscourt forehands off of a steady, not too weak, feed. You should try to hit good, firm forehands in the quarter court; that is to say, to the forehand side and beyond the serve line. What percentage go in? If, for instance, 18 out of twenty shots are good, then your percentage is 90%. In my experience, most players experience a rude awakening when they first measure this. I remember one player who felt his forehand was good and rather steady (his coach thought so, too). We first measured with a radar gun,

The Importance Of Consistency

and he was hitting well over 125 km/h. Then we fed balls to him with a ball machine at a speed of around 65 km/h (= not very fast). His actual percentage in the quarter court turned out to be only around 75%. This means that in a match, any rally with over 3 shots by him he would tend to lose!

Confidence and general mental state strongly affect consistency in a match situation. But the opposite is also quite true: a high level of consistency positively affects confidence and one's mental state, and understandably so. If you know down deep that you can not trust your shots, it's no wonder if you get nervous at key points in a match. What gets interpreted as mental problems often turn out to actually be problems with consistency, and when these problems are solved the mental problems also go away.

As we have seen, consistency is absolutely crucial for success in tennis, but at the same time tends to get neglected. Systematic practice dedicated to solely developing consistency is seldom done, let alone measured.

In the next chapter we are going to get into how one can develop consistency with some basic drilling. But before that, as a final note in this chapter, here is a chart showing mathematically how consistency affects rally length.

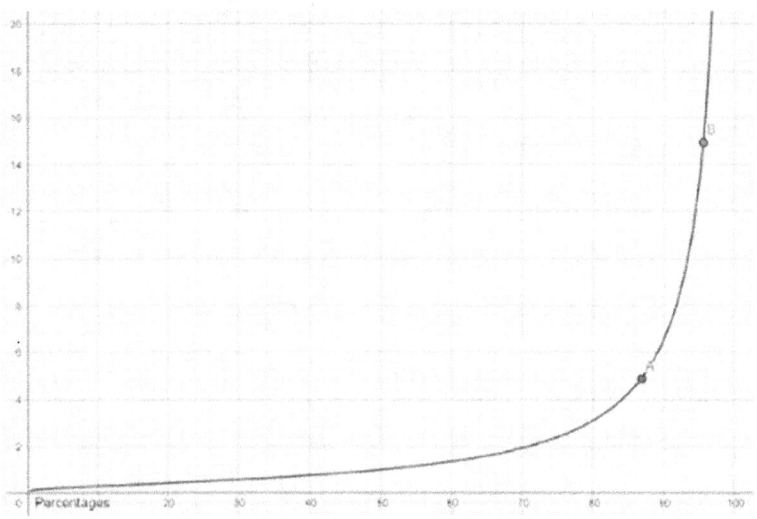

This is how the chart works: on the horizontal axis is the percentage of shots the player can hit without errors. On the vertical axis is how many shots in a rally the player on average can sustain without missing. At 80% we can see that the line on the chart corresponds to just barely over 3 shots, and certainly not 4. This chart also gives us a clear idea of where the critical points are. The curve bends sharply upward as soon as one goes above around 92%. At around 87% the consistency drops to less than 5 shot rallies being sustainable (point A). And at around 95% it shoots up to 15 shots, which would mean (adding the opponent's shots) that the player could hang in a 30 shot rally (point B). In the consistency drills in the next chapter we will aim for 95% accuracy, or in other words no more than one missed ball out of 20. Granted, this is a rather high figure, but in an actual match situation it would probably drop, so in practice we give it adequate margin.

CHAPTER 12

CONSISTENCY TRAINING

THIS CHAPTER IS ABOUT improving consistency. It contains specific drills that will get you there.

We covered in the previous chapter why consistency is so important and in the beginning of the book we talked a lot about "playing in the zone." It turns out that the consistency drills will also tend to be good drills for getting into the zone. You can kill two birds with one stone. Stating it more clearly: if you go through the consistency drills thoroughly and honestly and for long enough time you are almost guaranteed to end up in the mental state we call the zone. This drill, along with a later one called *"Concentration drill,"* are both on the surface very simple. At the same time they are also the most effective ones to guide you into the zone. Once there, the only problem will be to keep the state stable so that it holds up under pressure. The chapters dealing with emotions and how to handle destructive emotions will take care of that part. So take the consistency drills in this chapter seriously. They can make a huge difference in your game.

As we mentioned in the previous chapter, consistency means two different (but related) things. First, the ability to hit many high-quality shots without missing or committing unforced errors; second, the ability to keep stability at a high level without major dips over a long time period. In this chapter we will focus on the first definition: the ability to hit many shots of high quality and without missing.

What are the component parts that make up consistency? The first requirement for hitting a good shot is obviously that the player is where the ball is and in the proper position for the shot. So quickness around the court and good footwork.

Second, the form of the shot is correct. Irregular or jerky shots will tend to lower consistency. Part of this is also having a suitable amount of spin on the ball. Usually top spin helps with consistency (although there are a few players who seem able to defy this rule)

Third, hand-eye coordination or, in other words, ball perception. This skill is perhaps the one that takes the longest to develop and is to some degree what is called "talent." The earlier in life one starts with a ball sport the easier it is to acquire this skill. But even if the skill has not been fully mastered, it can still be markedly improved at a later stage through intense and focused practice.

Fourth, mental calm and stability. Once the proper technique and footwork have been mastered the most common reason for misses is mental. More about this point later.

So how do you improve consistency? The short and simple answer is: *practice hitting a lot of correct shots in a row*. Of course this is a rather unsatisfactory answer since what player in his right mind would intentionally do anything but hit shots correctly? Isn't that what practice is all about? Yes, indeed, that is what should happen in a practice session. But the problem is that it is seldom done in such a way as to get the full benefit. How so? To understand this, let's a look at what takes place when learning a shot.

At first the process is done at a fully conscious level, that is to say, you actively have to know what to do and deliberately make sure the body does it. Then, through practice, the shot gradually gets more and more automated until, at last, it becomes what is often referred to as "muscle memory," and you no longer need to think about *how* it's done, you just do it. In fact, if you even try to think about how you're doing it you tend to disrupt the shot. This is similar to how you once upon a time learned handwriting. You carefully and deliberately tried forming the letters, then gradually made it more and more automatic, until finally you could write without thinking of the motions. After that point in time your handwriting remained more or less constant, no matter how much you wrote.

It's the same way with shots in tennis. Once you have established the pattern, the shots remain more or less the same over the years and it can be very hard to change or modify them. It is therefore of the utmost importance that you form the shots correctly to begin with.

In the chapter *"Understanding the Principles of Training"* we covered rather thoroughly how to build correct technique and how the process is similar to learning handwriting. From that information it should be clear why "normal" practice may not be as effective as possible in building consistency, and – more importantly – how we might optimize consistency training.

Let's do a short review of some of the points made:

First of all, it is absolutely vital that the shots are correctly formed to begin with. This means that there should be no disturbances interfering with the process. Imagine, for instance, what would happen if you tried to learn writing, but someone continuously moved the paper around in front of you. This is literally what tends to happen in tennis. What moves? The ball, of course. So you're trying to groove your shot and find the proper form, but the object you're hitting moves all the time! Tennis is all about hitting a moving ball, so ultimately there is no way around this. But you can *gradually* introduce a moving ball and little by little adjust the speed and difficulty of the incoming shot, disturbing the swing as little as possible while learning the shot.

These two points are at the core of effective consistency practice:
- Focus very narrowly on one specific shot (and just one specific version of that shot).
- Only gradually increase the difficulty of the incoming ball so as to not disturb the proper execution of the shot.

A very common mistake in tennis is to think that the cause of all errors is an incorrect swing. You see this even at the highest professional level. A player misses a shot and then right afterward repeats the "wrong" swing or "rehearses" a right swing as if this would get to the root of the problem and correct the error. The real reason for the error, however, is usually that the player was slightly out of position or slightly mistimed the shot. Why? Because the incoming ball was difficult, or perhaps (and we will get to this problem soon) an inner mental disturbance affected the shot. The miss and "wrong" swing was merely a symptom of this underlying cause.

The same thing can often be seen at the beginner level. Here is a typical scenario. The player is practicing forehands. The coach feeds balls to the player. In the mind of the coach the feed might seem easy, but to the player it's very difficult. Consequently, mistakes are made. The coach verbally corrects all these. "Hit up on the ball." "Do proper follow-through." "Step into the shot." The real problem is that the player has trouble estimating the ball and this throws off the swing. To make matters worse (I don't know how many times I have seen this) the player is trying to hit a forehand with a continental grip and has developed tennis elbow, so is wearing a brace. The coach has never bothered correcting this. This sad scenario goes on for lesson after lesson.

How long should it take to learn a proper forehand and to be able to hit it with consistency? The swing itself (without the pesky problem of a ball) should not take more than a couple of hours at most. Being able to hit it with an extremely slow ball incoming (it can even be dropped right in front of the player) maybe 3 more hours. Then, gradually working up to full speed with consistency and precision is where the long haul comes in. Thousands of balls for sure. But if the player is started with a swing that is a bit off, and if gradual progress with the incoming ball is not adhered to, with strict focus on only one shot, the answer to the question "how long will it take" is unfortunately: forever!

Fundamentally, developing a shot and consistency is very much a question of being able to estimate a ball accurately so that the swing will meet the ball at the exact right time and place, in other words, ball perception/hand-eye coordination. This fact should never be underestimated. As a player increases his level in tennis this is one of the main things that is improved upon, of course also along with physical development of strength, speed and endurance, tactics. It is also one of the main things that is developed with consistency training. For further confirmation of this, consider the following points:

A top-level player practically never misses or mishits a shot when warming up, i.e., when the ball is hit with a moderate pace. A serve, on the other hand, which is hit at high speed (like more than 225 km/h) almost never comes back and is rarely hit with a "correct" swing.

When a player has a particularly good day or is in the zone you often hear him comment on how well he was seeing and timing the ball that day. In other words, perception is the underlying cause for playing well.

Structured and systematic consistency training helps raise the overall speed level at which the player is consistent and can hit without errors. The basic principles of consistency training remain the same regardless of the player's level. The only difference is how the parameters are set.

But enough with theory. Here is a practical description of how it is done.

The drilling starts with a realistic estimate of where the player is at. What is his/her level? What needs to be improved? Based on

this we set the general parameters. Specifically: what power level are we aiming at, and what level of precision do we demand?

In the following example the player was at an advanced level, playing futures but not yet challenger. The shot we decided to focus on was forehand crosscourt. The goal was to hit the ball firmly and with good top spin into the quarter court (beyond the serve line and to the deuce court side). The power level we aimed at was 125 km/h.

Next, we gradually work our way from very easy feeds to full power incoming balls hit by a sparring partner. In the beginning, the ball is literally just dropped in front of the player while working on grooving the shot, meaning that we find the exact and correct form/swing for the shot without any difficulty at all from the incoming shot. We keep a constant look at the success rate. Does the ball hit the quarter court? What % goes in? If the % sinks below 65%, we go back to a lower difficulty. If it reaches 95%, we go to the next higher difficulty of incoming ball. Below is a chart for structuring the drill.

	Technique				Mental
	Percent success rate				
FEED	60%	70%	80%	90%	95%
Sparring partner, full speed					
Ball machine oscillating					
Ball machine full speed					
Ball machine easy					
Feed by racquet					
Thrown from distance					
Tossed easy or dropped	**FORM** of shot perfected				

The drill is done row by row. Each row is taken to 95% success rate within the quarter court and at the designated speed of 125 km/h. So, for instance, the level of "Feed by racquet" is continued until 95% success rate is achieved before going to ball machine.

Note, the first line deals only with forming the shot. The feed is the easiest possible and the level is continued until the shot is perfectly grooved.

Also note that for each level, working from 65% up to 90% is mostly a matter of perfecting the technique. Thereafter, from 90%–95%, the difficulty becomes mostly mental.

At around 90% consistency you will begin to notice some very interesting mental phenomena. Up until then they already exist but compared to the mechanical errors are too insignificant to be worth bringing up. In normal drilling situations the coach usually changes to a different drill by the time the player loses interest or becomes mentally tired. With consistency drilling we take quite the opposite approach. As we all know, when trying to strengthen a physical muscle through, for instance, weight training, the gain only starts taking place when the limit of what the body can do is stretched beyond its normal capabilities. At this point the body sort of gets the message and starts adapting by growing the muscle bigger. With mental training it works the same way. Only when you stretch the mental demand beyond what the person can normally handle do you start seeing improvement.

It seems that the brain hates doing the exact same thing over and over. To escape such inconvenience, the brain has all kinds of tricks to get the person to quit. One is tiredness or boredom. Another one is irritation. Yet another one might be a feeling of compulsion to do something else (sort of like an itch that absolutely must be scratched). You can see the same thing in matches. Some players seem incapable of sustaining a simple cross-court rally for any amount of time; they simply *have* to do something drastic after a while. At the very top, players have mostly managed to master this urge, and patiently await the correct time to make a move. Djokovic is a perfect example. He can sustain a backhand rally almost indefinitely without missing or without feeling the need to do something else UNTIL – and that's a very important point – until there is an opening that he can take advantage of, at which point he doesn't hesitate. Such phenomena can be seen comparing players at challenger level and regular ATP. They do not have the same patience and feel the need to do something drastic (often at the wrong time with the wrong shot).

What happens if you just doggedly go on doing the drill above and simply ignore the signals from the brain that you should quit? Surprisingly, they disappear! Once you have shown "who's the boss" you will not get these feelings again and you will be able to drill with interest and without mental fatigue for as long as you desire. But beware, sometimes the signals to quit or change can be quite strong. I have heard players experience feelings like being hypnotized or almost going unconscious. It's not uncommon to have players feel like the lines are starting to bend in front of their eyes. The remedy in either case is to just continue until it goes away. The coach has a very big role at this stage. He needs to explain to the player what is happening and that it is actually a good thing, because now we are making headway on improving mental abilities.

You will also notice at this stage how incredibly sensitive the body is to thoughts. The player might successfully hit maybe 15 shots in a row and then suddenly start missing. When asked what happened he might say "I had the thought *I'm doing really good* and then I started missing." Or he might start worrying and likewise start missing. Even the thought "I should not be thinking" can trigger missing. Or if you tell the player that he needs to successfully hit 20 in a row (or 19 out of 20, that is) and he is getting close to success, then suddenly misses the last ball. This is the same kind of phenomena you see when a player tries to serve out a match or tries to hold serve after just breaking. The thoughts are more or less automatic and beyond the player's voluntary control.

As you can see from the numbers in the previous chapter, the difference between 90% and 95% is the difference between winning and losing at the top level. Here we see one obvious reason why tennis is such a mental game. No matter how well you have drilled your shots, even slight thoughts can disturb them and make you miss. And unless you have drilled your way through this unfortunate fact you are at risk in matches.

So what do you do to get through this last stage? We have already mentioned that "trying not to think" is just another way of disturbing the game. Here is what seems to work the best: just let the thoughts be and don't fight against them. The very act of fighting tends to make them stronger. Accept them and OBSERVE them. Then try to just relax your mind and keep your attention on the ball. After a while (which, I'm sorry to say, can sometimes be a very long while) the thoughts go away. At this point the player will suddenly just hit the ball and reach a state of inner calm not unlike what is called *the zone*. If you ask the player what he was doing that seemed to work, the answer is almost always the same: NOTHING, I was just hitting the ball.

Going back to the earlier chapter where we talked about Federer's match against Nadal in Australian Open, we hear the same words to describe this state. JUST HITTING THE BALL. Not worrying, not thinking. Just being there.

The various mental phenomena listed above will now be gone, seemingly having just evaporated, and a feeling of pleasure and alertness will set in.

And that's when the drill is done.

What's next? Obviously hitting cross-court forehands off a nice feed is not an end-all. We need to go through all shots in a similar manner. Then we combine them. Then maybe make the target area smaller and mix up the shots. Finally, hitting against a sparring partner of similar or higher skill level while still achieving the desired 95% consistency. You get the idea.

Long before this final level is reached, though, marked improvements will be seen in the player's consistency and match play. An added benefit is that practice in general will become more effective since the concentration level has gone up as well as the player's ability to maintain interest and mental intensity for prolonged time periods.

One final aspect that needs to be covered is how to set the parameters (i.e., incoming ball difficulty, target area to hit, power of shot hit and how much motion around the court). It all depends on the level of the player. As a rule of thumb, one should never set the parameters so strict that the player has less than 65% success rate. The reason is that if a shot is hit incorrectly, this too gets programmed in "muscle memory," so the player then is learning to hit the shot wrong. And the final success rate (except for serve drills, which is a separate chapter) should always be 95%. In the beginning, regardless of the player's general skill level, it is common to have to go back to almost zero pace of the incoming ball until the shot is properly grooved. This removes all other difficulties and distractions and puts the focus solely on the form.

As a general principle the drill should be difficult, but not too difficult, for the best results.

The quality of coaching during this drill is very important and makes a big difference.

At first glance this drill may seem overly simple. But make no mistake about it, the simple things are often the most powerful, and this drill is no exception. I once had a player do this type of drill and nothing else for two entire weeks 2-3 hours a day. Prior to this he was ranked 116 in the world. Within half a year he was ranked in the top 20s. The difference? Before the drill he had a very powerful forehand but lacked consistency and aim. After the drill he had both power and consistency. He made some other changes as well (I can't credit all of it to the drill), but this was a major contributing factor.

Do not underestimate the power of consistency drilling!

CHAPTER 13

ABOUT FEEDS

The importance of easy feeds
The importance of difficult feeds

A PLAYER NORMALLY FACES two types of feeds (incoming balls) when practicing. One is where the coach feeds balls out of a basket, hitting them lightly to the player. The other is where the player hits against a practice partner of comparable skill level. There is nothing inherently wrong with either method, but if the hitting is limited to only these two types of feeds, the progress is severely limited. Why?

As we learned in a previous chapter, when building technique and grooving in new shots, it is extremely important that the incoming ball – the feed – is constant and not too difficult, which is to say that it does not disturb the form of the shot or cause too many failures. For that reason, feeding from a basket might already be too difficult in the beginning stages. It might be necessary to, for instance, just toss the ball to begin with, and then gradually increase the difficulty. At the more difficult end of the spectrum there is also a limiting factor. You simply cannot feed a ball from a basket with sufficient power to provide a full challenge. If you think about it, you realize that balls similar to feeds almost never occur in a real match. So both at the high end of difficulty as well as the low end, the "one-feed-fits-all" approach is not ideal. Here is a picture illustrating the situation.

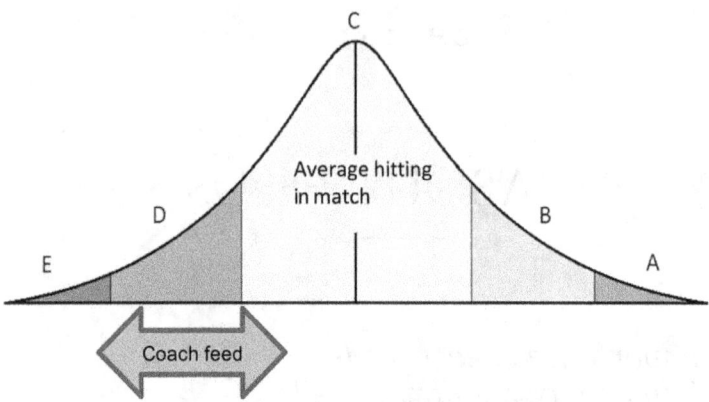

The bell curve shows various difficulty levels. Section C in the middle is the average level of difficulty in match play. Section E and D to the left show the level of difficulty needed when learning a new shot (= very easy). This level hardly ever happens in a match unless the opponent has totally missed. But this level is nonetheless needed in practice when learning or improving technique. Sections B and A to the right illustrate shots that are more difficult than the average. As we can see from the diagram, most shots in match-play are somewhere around average difficulty (60% of them or so). A few might be easier, providing an opportunity to attack; a few are more difficult requiring effective defense.

Looking further at the picture, we see a block arrow marking the general range of difficulty of a ball feed from a coach. It immediately becomes obvious that the player misses a large part of the range of difficulty in practice, both the very easy level and the extra difficult one. The consequences of this are two-fold. First, the learning process takes longer than necessary due to the exaggerated level of difficulty in the beginning stages. Second, and perhaps even more problematic, the player does not get to practice defending against really challenging shots. Of course, during sparring sessions with a player of comparable skill level, the more difficult shots will come from time to time. But not in a regular and structured fashion, which de facto means literally no practice on these.

In matches we see that players rarely miss shots in the average (yellow) zone of difficulty. Mostly the misses occur in the green zones. Are there exceptions? Absolutely. One of the things that are so remarkable about the very top ranked players is their ability to deal with extremely difficult balls coming at them. Take for example Djokovic's ability to reach and successfully return balls way beyond the sidelines. Or Federer's ability to take even very forcing shots on the up-bounce.

How does one become able to deal with such challenges? Talent? Yes, probably. But, more importantly, through training on those specific shots rather than just random hitting.

The more difficult shots and situations should be drilled systematically and deliberately. This might take some thinking and organizing. How do you set up drilling for hitting out-wide forehands on the run? How do you arrange for hitting a desperate almost out-of-reach forehand slice to recover in the rally? How do you set up drilling for handling getting bombed with a 150 km/h forehand? It's well worth the time and effort to construct and go through this type of drills though. The learning phase will speed up, and mastery of the game's extreme situations and challenges is made possible.

CHAPTER 14

NEGLECTED SKILLS

Peter Lundgren

I SOMETIMES GET ASKED what I think gets neglected in tennis training. What skills? What aspects of technique?

Obviously it varies from player to player and from coach to coach. I do see some common trends though.

Serve return. Arguably the second most important shot in tennis. Yet you rarely see players practice it for any length of time in an organized format. With one exception. This one might surprise some of you. I have trained not only ATP players (i.e., men) but also WTA players (women). One thing I quickly noticed was that when women practice serving their sparring partner is on the other side returning. With men, the player on the other side usually also serves. I also noticed that women often are stronger at serve returns than men. You may argue that this is because men serve harder, and, yes, they do. However, even in mixed doubles the women are surprisingly good at returning the serve from the man on the opposing team.

Volley. Often too little practice on volley. In matches this causes the players to hesitate going to the net. I have run into this with several of the players I trained. Safin, for one, seldom went to the net even though he had such tremendously good hands and long reach covering the net. It made a big difference in his game after we put in systematic practice on net play.

Consistency. As covered in previous chapters, consistency is a skill in itself. It's made up of several parts: correct technique, good footwork, endurance and speed around the court, for instance. Finally, probably the most important ingredient, is the mental part. Being consistent is mentally hard and requires mental consistency training drills to break through. Doing a drill for a long time gets mentally tiring, as if the brain protests. When I was in the earlier part of my career I was coached by Birger Folke. He was a real stickler for consistency and precision. He made us hit shot after shot and we had to hit a small square in the corner of the court 25 times before he let us off the hook. Some of the players reacted very strongly and absolutely HATED it. I myself managed to suffer through it, and I can definitely say that it served me well in future matches. I knew I could stay in a rally, and I knew I could trust those shots. Players at lower levels sometimes do not appreciate just how consistent the top players are. The book covers it, with statistics and all, in a previous chapter. But here is an example I myself witnessed.

At US open one year, Wawrinka and Djokovic were doing a morning training hour together on the center court. I had brought 8 balls for Wawrinka and Djokovic, too, had brought 8 balls. They start warming up, hitting balls from the baseline. And hitting and hitting. I had never seen anything like it. Sick! They just didn't miss. Not at all. After what seemed like an eternity, perhaps 10 or 15 minutes, I actually had to intervene. Why? The ball was completely worn out and I had to throw it away. Meanwhile the 15 remaining balls had remained untouched in my charge. Now that's consistency for you.

CHAPTER 15

THE IMPENETRABLE CASTLE

Training with Björn Borg

In this chapter we get a rare glimpse of how one of the most dominant players of all time trains, his consistency and intensity.

Peter Lundgren

Björn literally means Bear in Swedish and Borg means castle or stronghold. What a befitting name! Björn as a player was strong as a bear and utterly impenetrable—like playing against a wall or trying to break into a castle.

In late 1983 and onward I had the privilege of being one of Borg's practice partners. I'm intentionally saying "one of" because Borg needed more than one opponent to get any sense of a challenge. I never officially competed against Björn, and his tennis career has been amply documented elsewhere. What I can contribute is a bit of insight into what it was like to practice against him and to know him personally as a friend.

Björn had just announced his retirement from the professional tour in 1983. But he still wanted to keep in shape and to practice regularly. Not sure why. I mean, he certainly didn't need money and he had absolutely nothing left to prove. I suppose a mix of the love of the game and, as I said, wanting to stay in shape and to have something of interest to do. His tennis record was unprecedented with 11 grand slam wins already at his early retirement at age 26. It was thought at the time that his Roland Garros record was insurmountable and also his series of "Channel slams" (winning Roland Garros and Wimbledon consecutively within the same year). He had single-handedly changed the face of tennis from a sort of snobbish conservative sport to a wildly popular phenomenon reaching all audiences, both old and young. And as a consequence, he had contributed to making tennis much more profitable for the players. All on the pro tour these days owe Björn a debt of gratitude.

Björn had been my idol growing up as a tennis player. He was the front figure and driving force behind what was known as the Swedish tennis wonder. Just how big and dominant Swedish tennis had become internationally was brought home to me rather forcefully when, as a tennis professional ranked in the top 30, I was not good enough to even qualify for the Swedish Davis Cup team. Those were the days.

Imagine my excitement, then, when suddenly I was allowed to practice with my idol. Who could ask for more as a budding tennis professional?

So what was it like? Let's start with a practice session, such as they usually were. I arrive well before time—I hate being late. But I found Björn already there having coffee. He would usually show up 45 minutes or an hour before practice in order to be fully ready.

Next, warmup. Warmup with Björn was not like warmups with anyone else (or any warmups I had experienced previously in my training). It wasn't that he was hitting overly hard. He wasn't. The shots were just firm and steady. Never bad. And, most importantly, HE NEVER MISSED. And when I say never, I mean NEVER. The balls just kept coming back, over and over and over and over. Finally, they were all on my side of the net. So what does Björn do? Runs over to my side and picks them all up before I could even get to it. Boy, did I feel like a slouch then! He liked long warmups so we would go at it for about 20-25 minutes. Perhaps he would miss a ball or two during this time, but not more. Being that I had the privilege of practicing with Borg I would do my absolute best to focus and not miss. I felt a lot of pressure to perform and to provide good sparring for Björn. But try as I may, I could never keep up with him and inevitably I would be the first one to miss.

A 20-minute warmup with Björn was like having played at least two sets of match play against any other good opponent. You were just wiped out and felt like you had been run over by a train. And this was just the warmup! Next was match play.

Björn only wanted to play sets. He wasn't interested in doing drills and such. If warmup was tough, then match play was even tougher. As I mentioned, Björn at this tim had nothing left to prove and, besides, these matches were not "real" matches. Nothing at stake, just keeping in shape and having fun sort of. Nonetheless, to Björn, there was no goofing around. He was fully intent on winning every set and every game and point. He would never let up. It seems like Björn simply did not have it in him to play at less than 100% intensity. It was awesome to behold the mental power and presence of him at the other side of the net. It must have been pure hell for other players to face him in actual competition.

His mental focus did not show outwardly as any kind of effort or strain. In a sense you didn't even notice it. But as play went on you could feel it as an unstoppable force which gradually wore you down. And if the match ever got even or critical, he could step it up a notch. We would sometimes just for the fun of it trash talk a bit at changeovers. If the score was, say, 6-5 in my favor he could say "OK, now I'm breaking serve." Then he proceeded to do just that. Frustrating. But at the same time an incredible learning experience.

It seemed like his physical and mental energy was absolutely inexhaustible. After he was done with me (and I was well-baked and "done" to a point of having to go home and collapse on my bed) the next practice partner would take over. I think that's maybe why he would sometimes appear to rush a bit between points. He had so much energy. One point barely ended before the next one started. It also showed in how he would collect the balls between points. If he, for instance, had served and volleyed and I had missed into the net, he would immediately run OVER TO MY SIDE and pick up the ball! I was told by Per "Pelle" Hjertquist, who used to practice with Borg when he was still active on the tour, that back then Borg would regularly go through, not just two players, but THREE in the very same day! After wearing down the first one to a point of complete exhaustion ("they had to carry him out on a stretcher") the next one would come in and so forth.

I recently asked Björn about physical training. I myself had been inactive for a while and needed to get back in shape. I asked him what he would do. He adamantly said, "never the gym." Get out and run in the forest. That's what I would do. He never went to the gym. Sort of Rocky Balboa style.

On that note, it's worth mentioning what an extraordinary physical specimen Borg was. Not only endurance, but also speed and strength. In 1976 he took part in an event in Vichy, France, called "Superstars" where various top athletes would compete in sports not their own. Essentially a decathlon. Borg came in first place. Won the 100-m dash (12.3 sec), won soccer skills, won kayaking, won table tennis, 4thplace pistol shooting, 3rd place cycling, and to everyone's surprise won and beat Guy Drut at the 600-m steeple chase. Guy won the 110m hurdles in the Olympics the very same year!

There were a few oddities with Björn's training and methods. Once, for instance, he had been practicing with Patrik Albertsson. This was in London, just before one of his comeback attempts. Patrik had been worked out hard practicing with Borg (read "beaten to a pulp") and said he was so tired he would need to take a day off. Borg said, "let me show you how to fix it." So they went to Björn's hotel room, where Björn filled up the bathtub with scalding hot water. In London they did not have temperature regulation, so the hot water was REALLY hot. Patrik dipped his toe into the water and said there was no way he could do this. Too hot! Borg insisted that he just had to "get in there, or else you won't be able to play tomorrow." Finally he did, screaming in pain. And somehow it seemed to have worked. The next day he felt OK and managed to practice just fine. Another oddity was Björn's (or should I say Lennart Bergelin's) famous "massages" (massages is in quotation marks, because a more appropriate word would probably be "torture"). Björn's coach, Lennart Bergelin, would regularly give Björn massages. Lennart was a strong man with big powerful hands. Pelle Hjertquist once got to experience this. After a practice session he was offered a "treatment." Bergelin massaged him at full force, finding all his pressure points, and laying into them with all his might until Pelle absolutely screamed in pain, while Bergelin yelled "take that you little bastard!" No mercy. But Borg had gotten used to this and could take the hour-long massages without complaining.

My tennis, of course, improved a lot during this time period. Borg was helpful not only on court as a practice partner and mentor, but also in other ways. I'm aware that the press over the years has written quite a lot of negative things about Björn. My view of him is the exact opposite. He is a generous, genuine and very friendly person. I'd like to take the opportunity here to share some of my experiences with Björn:

One day in 1984, after training, Björn told me he was going to Brazil for an exhibition match. He asked me if I wanted to come along. "Of course," I said. Björn arranged the whole trip and even let me bring my girlfriend. We spent 10 wonderful days in Brazil with everything paid and I also got to play some tennis matches against the local talents. A great learning experience. Another example. In 1986 Björn played an exhibition match at some sort of promotional event in Stockholm. At this time he arranged sponsoring for me, with a traveling coach. Basically took care of me for most of 1986 and enabled me to travel and train.

As fate would have it, many years later I had the good fortune of being one of the people helping Federer break many of Björn's records. In his time Björn was regarded as the GOAT (greatest of all time). Now it's Federer. What are the odds that one person should be so lucky as to get to be in close proximity to both these rare examples of human achievement? I feel awe and gratitude for having had the privilege of witnessing these two masters firsthand.

So what have I learned? I can say that one trait they share is a magical, almost mystical, mental strength and ability. I think this is perhaps the most important key to success. The mental part.

Björn and I still keep in touch regularly, and I regard him as one of my very best friends.

PART THREE

In the next few chapters we will cover the following topics:

- Understanding emotions and how they affect tennis
- Review of methods for dealing with unwanted emotions
- Specific methods for handling unwanted emotions
- Final words on bad days and the zone

CHAPTER 16

UNDERSTANDING EMOTIONS

ONE OF THE MOST DIFFICULT aspects of tennis is the fact that emotions affect the game so strongly and gaining control of them can be immensely difficult. Nervousness, for instance, can in a split second completely ruin the ability to hit a tennis ball. We see it often even at the very highest levels and with experienced players, for example when they have to serve for the match and suddenly they double fault after a whole match of no such errors. Or, to take another example, the emotion of anger. It can completely wreck a player's game for several points after the outburst, sometimes even for an entire set or match, if the player is unable to let go. To make things worse, the problem does not only concern negative emotions. Positive emotions are also able to distract and destroy, such as when a player is ahead and enthusiastically lets his thoughts drift to the possibility of actually winning and what might take place then suddenly: WHAM! The game falls apart and nothing works anymore. I know of situations where a player has been up 6-0, 5-0, serving for the match and then suddenly everything fell apart and the player lost.

Keeping troublesome emotions under control is one of the greatest challenges in competitive tennis. This ability alone is sometimes equated with mental toughness, that's how central it is in the game. In this chapter we will try to analyze why and how emotions affect the game so strongly, and why it can be so hard to control them. Towards the end of the chapter we will look at some general options for what we can do to gain control over the emotions. But first, let's take a closer look at the problem.

What would you guess is the percentage of points won for the very best players, such as Nadal, Federer or Djokovic? People I ask usually guess somewhere around 60 or 70 percent.

The large chart on the next page shows actual official ATP statistics for several players, including their % of points won over their career (the last line on the chart). Note some very interesting facts. First of all, even for the top players, the actual figure is not 60% or 70%, but rather a mere 54% (55% for Nadal). What this means, putting it in perspective, is that if 20 points were played, and the players were absolutely evenly matched, then the score would be 10-10. With a 55% win rate, only ONE SINGLE POINT would go in favor of the better player rather than being evenly distributed between the two. Yet despite this tiny advantage, virtually every single grand slam over the last 20 or so years has been won by one of the three names above, or they have at least been in the final. If we then compare them to some of the other really good players in the statistics chart, we can see that they are not much behind in % points won. Even so, 51% is apparently not enough to reach the very top.

Looking closely at the statistics, we see that a 54% *points won* ratio results in 59%-60% *games won*. This in turn leads to a rather astonishing 83% or so of *matches won* (see chart below). Putting it differently: if you are good enough to take *even one more point out of twenty* than your opponent, then you will win in the vast majority of your matches.

Career winning %, top players

Name	Career winning %	Career titles	Career win/loss
Rafael Nadal	83.2	85	992/201
Novak Djokovic	83.1	81	924/188
Bjorn Borg	82.4	66	654/140
Roger Federer	82.1	103	1242/271

MIND OVER TENNIS

Singles Service Record

	Federer	Djokovic	Nadal	Sampras	Isner	Karlovic	Agassi	Zverev	Tsitsipas	Kyrgios	Thiem
Aces	11.478	6.354	3.828	8.858	13.411	13.728	4.082	3.846	2.143	3.884	2.705
Double Faults	2.759	2.638	2.037	3.009	1.633	2.452	2.108	1.891	670	913	1.287
1st Serve	62%	65%	68%	69%	66%	63%	65%	62%	66%	60%
1st Serve Points Won	79%	74%	72%	81%	79%	83%	73%	75%	76%	77%	74%
2nd Serve Points Won	57%	55%	57%	53%	56%	53%	54%	50%	55%	53%	53%
Break Points Faced	6.459	5.9	6.239	3.751	2.866	2.648	4.764	2.584	1.545	1.247	2.707
Break Points Saved	67%	66%	67%	68%	71%	71%	65%	61%	65%	66%	63%
Service Games Played	18872	14350	14615	10641	10315	9614	10512	5783	3921	3521	5841
Service Games Won	89%	86%	86%	89%	92%	92%	84%	82%	86%	88%	83%
Total Service Points Won	70%	67%	67%	69%	72%	73%	66%	66%	68%	69%	66%

Singles Return Record

	Federer	Djokovic	Nadal	Sampras	Isner	Karlovic	Agassi	Zverev	Tsitsipas	Kyrgios	Thiem
1st Serve Return Points Won	32%	34%	34%	29%	22%	21%	32%	31%	29%	24%	30%
2nd Serve Return Points Won	51%	55%	55%	51%	42%	40%	56%	51%	49%	47%	50%
Break Points Opportunities	11.948	10.114	10.799	6.164	3.451	2.707	7.679	3.479	2.027	1.439	3.52
Break Points Converted	41%	44%	45%	41%	30%	30%	43%	42%	40%	39%	39%
Return Games Played	18475	13960	14472	10422	10205	9589	10516	5793	3834	3508	5854
Return Games Won	27%	32%	34%	24%	10%	9%	32%	25%	21%	16%	24%
Return Points Won	40%	42%	42%	38%	28%	28%	42%	38%	36%	33%	38%

Totals

	Federer	Djokovic	Nadal	Sampras	Isner	Karlovic	Agassi	Zverev	Tsitsipas	Kyrgios	Thiem
% Total Games Won	58.3%	59.3%	60.1%	56.8%	51.2%	50.1%	58.0%	53.4%	54.8%	52.1%	53.4%
% Total Points Won	54%	54%	55%	54%	51%	50%	53%	52%	52%	51%	51%

If you think about it, these figures are a bit odd. With a winning ratio of just above 50% points we are very close to pure chance. A coin toss, so to speak. Based on this we might logically predict a similar overall match winning percentage (about 50 %), but clearly this is not so. How is this possible? How can a 55% *point* win ratio result in an 83% *match* win ratio?

Tennis, it is often said, is all about winning the **important** points. The break points, the match points and so forth. For some reason, the very best players seem to be able to pull it off when it matters the most. Is it that they have some sort of magical "superpower" they can turn on when they need it? Perhaps. But I think, based on personal experience and match analysis with various players, that the most common explanation is that the better players are able to maintain their level of play under pressure, while others tend to slightly drop their level in such situations. I'm not denying that you indeed do see some miraculous points now and then from the top players. But it's by no means an iron-clad rule. It's just that they tend to not make mistakes or lose focus when they need it. A few points, or even a single point, can make all the difference in a match. Case in point: the recent US open final (2020) between Alexander Zverev and Dominic Thiem. Despite a 2-set lead, serving for the match in the third, and leading with a break in the fifth, Zverev still lost by, as Boris Becker put it, by ONE point! By all accounts, it appeared that Zverev had an insurmountable lead and played better than Thiem. What happened? Perhaps a clue might be that in the beginning of the match Zverev served 140mph at times, compared to the 5th set tiebreak where he served a first serve at only 98mph. Wow!! And his second serve at match point crawled in at 68 mph!

What happened? Or more importantly, what is it that causes players to play worse right at those times when it matters the most?

The performance level in tennis can, of course, drop for a number of reasons. Getting tired. Injury. Opponent figures out a way of tactically neutralizing one's game and so forth.

While all of these alternatives are possible, the fact is that the underlying reason in the vast majority of cases is one single thing: EMOTIONS.

Emotions can be every bit as devastating as a sprained ankle or a broken string and they can impinge on play with lightning speed.

The problems of emotions are of course not something unique to just tennis; they tend to be a deciding factor in all sports. Not only that, emotions also tend to be a problem in life in general. People are plagued by things like depression, shame, regret, jealousy, apathy, grief and various other negative emotions.

In tennis we can in, a way, consider ourselves fortunate when it comes to emotions. How so? Well, once on the court we are generally not affected in our game by more than a couple of types of negative emotions. Although their particular form of expression can vary from case to case, the emotions that negatively influence play can be summarized into just a few basic categories.

FEAR. In this category we include such phenomena as choking, hesitation, lack of confidence, being too timid, holding back and so on.

ANGER. In this category we include phenomena or situations such as upset over line calls, angry at umpire, weather, court conditions, the player's own mistakes and so on.

LOSS OF FOCUS/CONCENTRATION. Although this is not in itself an emotion, it is most usually caused by emotions. It can be one of the negative emotions, such as anger or fear, but it can also be driven by positive emotions, such as winning a set or thinking about how nice it might be to win the match.

The big question, then, is what to do about it. How can we get rid of negative emotions, or better yet avoid them altogether? Whole industries are built around offering such solutions. Pharmaceuticals, meditation, psychology, yoga, religion, mental coaching, even dieting and exercise just to mention a few. Which ones should we choose? Which ones work the best for our specific problem: tennis?

A good place to start would be to acquire a better understanding of the problem. What are emotions, really? How do they turn on and why? How come they are so hard to control? Sometimes just understanding the nature of a difficulty can help untangle it, and the more you understand it, the easier it will be to apply the various techniques and drills further on in the book. We will therefore be quite thorough in trying to analyze the nature of emotions and how they work. If you find the chapter too long it's totally OK to go right on to the various drills and techniques in the later chapters. But you might find it a bit harder to apply them successfully.

It turns out that a fair amount of research has been carried out on the subject. We will cover some of the relevant findings—those that are most applicable to tennis.

What are emotions really? And what are they for? We sometimes like to think that our thoughts (preferably logical and sane) govern our emotions, and emotions in turn govern our behavior. Is that "model" really true though? Research tends to point in a different direction. Psychologist Jonathan Haidt in his famous book *The Happiness Hypothesis* uses an analogy of an elephant and a rider. The rider represents our logical, reasoning, mind. The elephant represents our emotions. The rider might think he is in charge all the time. But the reality is that if he and the elephant disagree then they will go in the direction the elephant decides. The elephant is much stronger and bigger than the rider.

It's like that with our mind. The reasoning part is often quite powerless against the emotional forces. Did you ever get angry and regret it afterwards? Or perhaps indulge in eating something unhealthy? Or drink too much? Or procrastinate with getting something done that you knew logically should be done? I'm sure you can come up with your own examples of situations where your elephant won, regardless of what you, the rider, logically knew to be the correct action. And therein lies the rub. We know logically that negative emotions are not helpful and oftentimes not logical. Nonetheless they are there, and they overpower us.

Back to the first question. What are emotions really? We are so used to constantly having them or talking about them that we rarely, if ever, reflect on what they actually are. Let's take one common emotion, such as anger. What is it? What are the component parts? Far from a complete description, here are some of the common manifestations of anger: increased heart rate and blood pressure; increased muscle tension and often jerkiness of movement; faster breathing; less sensitivity to pain; raised voice; often an intense glare at the target of the anger; a desire or drive to attack or break/destroy something or someone. These things, we could say, describe roughly what happens to the elephant (the physical and emotional level). And what about the rider (the thinking and logical/reasoning level)? His thoughts are geared to creating insults, or attacking, and logical thinking itself is lessened or eliminated altogether. You could say that the rider has been recruited by the elephant to help with the elephant's quest for destruction and mayhem, driven by the emotional state of anger.

These manifestations of anger are not unique to humans. Most well-evolved animals (and certainly most mammals) share the same pattern. Sometimes with a few differences (such as showing teeth, etc.). Now we can ask ourselves, would nature have evolved such a pattern and used it for most animals if it didn't serve some kind of purpose forwarding survival? Obviously not. So at its root, this particular pattern must benefit the species and the individual somehow. How? And why?

I'm reminded here of a funny YouTube video: (https://www.youtube.com/watch?v=u2zgr_Gg11U) An old lady crosses the street on a crosswalk while a man sitting in a sportscar gets more and more impatient as the old lady slowly makes her way in front of him. He revs the engine and shows in various ways how displeased he is with her speed of movement. Finally the lady has had enough and hits the car with her purse. This sets off the airbag inside the car and hits the driver rather hard (as airbags do).

The airbag system is, as we know, constructed for the purpose of saving the driver's life in case of an accident. But in this case the system has misread the situation and goes off without real cause. The whole thing happens with lightning speed, so the driver has no chance whatsoever to react or stop the mechanism. The system must be that fast, though, because it is exactly meant to save a driver's life in a situation where logical thinking would be way too slow to prevent disaster. It's automatic and immediate.

Do you see the similarity to how emotions work? Has it, for instance, ever happened that you thought logically to yourself "I think it would be a good idea if I got angry now" or "I think a reasonable course of action at this point in time would be to break a racquet and yell at the umpire." Probably not. I would guess that the emotion, and concurrent action, just (like an airbag) took place by themselves and only afterwards did you reflect on it, and perhaps regret your outburst.

The emotion of anger, and the whole package that goes with it, is pre-programmed. You could say it's hard wired into the system, to use a computer analogy, and will unfold more or less completely when triggered by certain situations or events. The difference between our anger circuit and the air bag example is that our conscious thinking (the rider) can exert at least a certain measure of control over it. At least most people do. The anger circuit might trigger about as fast as an air bag, but fortunately it tends to unfold much slower, so there is time for the logical thinking of the person to intervene before someone gets hurt or killed.

The design of an air bag system and how it's supposed to help in a collision is quite clear. How about the emotion of anger and its various manifestations? How is this supposed to help anything? We can reasonably assume that its original and intended purpose is to be helpful in situations involving confrontation and conflict. In such situations we can see how less sensitivity to pain might be helpful. Likewise increased heart rate (giving more oxygen to the muscles for added strength). Increased loudness or growling might serve as a deterrent. Jerky motions might be a side effect of increased muscle tone or perhaps be helpful in a fist fight. Against the background of all this information we are almost ready to agree that anger and its various manifestations and even side effects are reasonable and workable.

Except for one thing. As any boxer or person practicing martial arts knows, anger is a sure ticket to losing a fight. You have to keep your mind cool and not get lost in emotions. If you get angry you no longer have your power of reasoning intact and will undoubtedly commit tactical or technical errors (like letting your guard down) in a fit of rage. The fact is that yes, you need to keep

your body active and energized. But at the same time you have to keep your head cool and your logical and reasoning powers fully intact.

Conclusion: anger is a hard-wired response that exists in almost identical form in all evolved animals. Once triggered, it manifests in the same way, regardless of the reason or the target of the anger. In a very primitive situation, the physical and other component parts of anger may help with survival. Especially if the animal in question has not evolved full reasoning powers or a workable fighting system. In that case a pre-programmed automatic and very fast response may be the only workable solution. It would indeed seem that this is the case, considering that the anger response has persisted in practically identical form in all higher species for millions of years.

But not in humans. Not in a modern environment. And for sure not in sports. Even though sports in many ways emulates primitive fighting situations, letting primitive emotions run the show is a guaranteed way to lose in most situations. And the same thing applies in regular day-to-day life. If you cannot control anger, even if provoked, and regularly get into fits of rage, you will most likely be a failure socially (and perhaps end up in anger management class).

Further conclusion: the anger mechanism is in most cases outdated and not workable in helping survival in modern society. Also, like an air bag system, in some situations it can be overly sensitive or outright misplaced. Anger is built for, and somewhat useful, in situations in nature where an animal is subjected to threat or danger. Does this apply to, for instance, the situation where a tennis player intends to hit the ball in the court and misses? Is anger helpful? Does he need a higher heart rate, a shutting down of reasoning powers, raised blood pressure, jerky muscle movements, a burning desire for destruction and mayhem, a raised voice, and perhaps a broken racquet?

The answer is obviously no. He is NOT in the jungle being attacked by, say, a lion. He *does* have reasoning powers, so there is no need for an automatic anger mechanism to take over. And yet...there is the broken racquet. Or the code violation penalty for yelling at the umpire or cursing out loud. The anger mechanism is, in this situation, unworkable, triggered by a threat that really isn't the kind of threat anger was designed for. Even so, it gets triggered and takes control. The "rider of the elephant" helplessly gets taken along by the rage and rampage of the wild animal.

We have so far just talked about one single emotion: anger. A similar analysis could be carried out for many others. Take for grief. This emotion, too, has a pre-programmed response and script. It tends to be a bit less primitive (which is to say it has evolved later) than anger and so does not appear to exist in certain less-evolved species (does a snake feel grief?) but is nevertheless a pre-set list of responses. My point here is that there is a plethora of human emotions. Most of them can be traced far back in evolution, and they tend to be quite automatic (like an air bag) and pre-set. They also, most importantly for our purposes, tend to directly influence the body in various ways. Most of these are destructive of the ability to play tennis, which is why we bring up the subject in this book.

These emotions come into play with a speed that is quite remarkable. One situation I often encounter is where a player somehow tends to miss easy put-away shots. The ball just sits there, ready for pouncing. The player has practiced the shot hundreds of times and has no difficulty executing it. Mysteriously he misses it in matches.

Why?

Investigating the matter closely you find that at the crucial moment – just as the ball is about to get hit—the player either becomes worried or, at the other end of the spectrum, says to himself "now I'm really going to hit the ball for a clear winner." Both reactions have the result of changing muscle tone. Fear of missing tends to lower it and hitting with exaggerated force tends to increase it. In either case, the end product is a missed shot. In practice sessions the shot has always been hit with just the right amount of force and muscle tension. The player has never practiced hitting it with exaggerated force or with no force, thus it fails. This change happens with astonishing speed. Even the short time it takes for the racquet to travel from the backswing to ball impact is long enough to completely change both the internal emotions and, consequently, how the muscles in the arm work.

So here we are. Emotions come in and disturb the game, lowering performance. They come as a pre-programmed package regardless of what type of situation may have triggered them. They cause various physical reactions as well as mental. They often overpower the player. The emotions themselves can be triggered by things that have little, or nothing, to do with the situations they were meant for in nature. And even when it happens to be the type of situation they were meant for, the reactions they cause are often not practical for the modern environment we live in.

The next question is what to do about it? How do we deal with this problem of destructive emotions getting in the way of the game?

Essentially we have two possible approaches. We can either try to strengthen the mind of the player to the point where he can control and overcome the negative emotions ("overpower the elephant") or we can try to avoid triggering the negative emotions

in the first place ("prevent the air bag from triggering"). Clearly, the second option would be the best. The problem with this approach, however, is that it can be complicated and difficult to achieve, therefore requiring a level of expertise and skill neither coach nor player might possess. The other option (getting control of the emotions) is simpler and, in many cases, within reach of the player himself without the need for expert help.

In practical terms, here is what we are looking at. Getting control of emotions by strengthening the mind of the player is often useful and workable for the various forms of anger and also for improving concentration so as to avoid lapses. It can include such methods as mindfulness, concentration drills, willpower training (see separate chapter on this) rituals, relaxation and breathing techniques, or the drills described in the chapter on consistency training.

Avoiding negative emotions altogether by making sure they are not triggered in the first place is, as mentioned above, a considerably more difficult approach, but if successful completely handles the problem. When it comes to emotions covered under the category we call FEAR, this approach can be the only one that actually works. Trying to suppress the fear or trying to move attention elsewhere generally fails to produce the desired result. Willpower training does not seem to bite on this type of problem. Nonetheless, some coaches seem to think that their players can overcome fear, tentativeness, and choking by just wanting to or by "listening to what their coach is telling them."

This second method (not triggering negative emotions in the first place) rests on the principle that emotional reactions in most cases are *learned*, not instinctive or "hard wired," to use computer terms. Let me explain. If someone suddenly comes up behind you and screams loudly then you will react and at least momentarily get scared. This is what I would call *instinctive*, which is to say it is not something you have to learn. Even a small child would react automatically. Same with such a thing as fear of heights. Quite automatic. Now on the other hand many people have a fear of guns and other weapons. This sort of fear only happens after learning that guns potentially are deadly. The fear of guns, at that moment, becomes connected to the more instinctive fear of death or injury, and thereby can trigger the same intense fear reaction. It should also be noted here that the mind continuously monitors the environment and interprets it. As soon as this interpretation detects a match between the learned fears and current events the fear reaction is triggered.

Most of the fear reactions we encounter in tennis (choking, nervousness, being overly careful or tentative) are of the learned type—obviously no one is born with a worry about just what side of a chalk line a furry yellow ball lands. So whenever we encounter a fear-type reaction in tennis, the *apparent* fear is triggered by and gets its power from an underlying *basic/instinctive* fear. The fear of hitting a serve at match point may at a more fundamental level be a fear of losing or making a public mistake. And beneath that might be a basic fear of losing position in the group (an instinctive fear) or maybe a fear of being ridiculed (also instinctive). The important point here is that the learned fear, which impacts tennis negatively and which we want to dispose of, is at a lower level connected to, and gets its power from, a basic instinctive fear.

This connection is possible to break! And when this is achieved the learned fear loses its power or altogether disappears. In other words, it is possible to "unlearn" the fear or to "re-learn" a better reaction to the current situation. In simple terms, this is accomplished by either backtracking to the moment the mental connection was made and through inspection and reconsidering the conclusions made at that point in time severing the tie or else possibly by re-evaluating the current situation so that it no longer gets interpreted as something worthy of reaction. Replacing nervousness with positive anticipation or excitement might be one example of what we are after. These methods can of course also work for other undesirable emotions, but as mentioned above, they can be difficult to apply. For more information on how to do this, please refer to the three chapters *Re-framing, Deep*

Analysis, and *Getting to the Source,* which specifically deal with such methods.

SUMMARY OF CHAPTER

1. Tennis matches are decided by very small margins.
2. Even a minor lapse can change the outcome of a match and usually is the determining factor in matches between players of similar skill levels.
3. The small lapses are most often caused by undesirable emotions interfering with play.
4. Emotions can almost instantly affect the physical body and interfere with performance.
5. Emotions are at the root survival mechanisms evolved over millions of years. They were built for primitive life in nature.
6. Emotions tend to overpower the intellect and logic.
7. Emotions cause both mental and physical reactions.
8. These reactions are often not workable in our modern environment. In fact, they can often have the exact opposite effect than the one intended.
9. Understanding how emotions work can somewhat alleviate their impact. But to really deal with them effectively requires a specialized approach.
10. It is possible to strengthen the mind through systematic and focused practice to a point where many of the unwanted emotions can be controlled.
11. In the most difficult cases, the emotional mechanisms themselves need to be severed altogether, thereby preventing the emotions from being triggered at all.
12. Point 11 is possible to achieve but may require specialized help.

CHAPTER 17

MENTAL MELTDOWN

Peter's Example

Peter Lundgren

HERE IS A PERSONAL EXAMPLE of how strongly even small emotional changes and tiny thoughts can impact performance and change the outcome of a match.

I was meeting Glenn Layendecker in the Australian Open 1991. I was so happy because I had managed to qualify for the main draw, and if I could beat Glenn could possibly get to play against Patrick McEnroe later on in the tournament.

Everything was going my way. I won the first set 6-3. Second set was even better 6-1. I was on a roll. In the third set I was up 5-4 serving at 40-0. Sure win, right?

Not so.

A tiny thought comes in "what if I lose this lead?" Sure enough, I started playing a bit more carefully and before I knew it I had missed several passing shots and Glenn broke serve, 5–5.

Not a catastrophe, I thought. I'm still two sets up. So we start the next game. He holds. 6 – 5 to Layendecker. My turn to serve. Now I can't stop thinking "what if I get broken again?" I couldn't stop my attention from going back to the previous break of serve and letting it go. Sure enough, he manages to break my serve one more time and takes the set 7–5.

The rest of the match proceeds the same way. I just can't get the thoughts and emotions out of my mind.

In the end I lost 3-6, 1-6, 7-5, 6 – 3, 6 – 4.

Emotions can be quite overpowering.

Thoughts, even tiny ones, can trigger them.

CHAPTER 18

REVIEW OF METHODS FOR DEALING WITH UNWANTED EMOTIONS

DEALING WITH UNWANTED EMOTIONS is not a problem unique to tennis. It is very much a factor in all sports, and indeed permeates all human life. Consequently, a multitude of solutions, or should I say methods that *claim* to be solutions, have been invented.. In several countries up to 10% of the population uses medication to handle depression, for instance . Imagine how many people must have problems with feeling depressed if as many as 10% went so far as to take medication for the problem! Then we have such things as yoga, meditation, self-help books, religion, psychology and psychiatry, and life coaches. Some of these methods may claim to have a different purpose than dealing with emotions (for instance religions), but would anyone get involved with them if they didn't make you feel better and instead made you depressed or angry?

A list of the various types of emotional problems people have would be very long indeed. If we pay a little attention, we can see these all around us every day: grief, anger, depression, hate, jealousy, just to mention a few.

In tennis we can consider ourselves lucky in a way because, as discussed, there are only a couple emotions that cause most of the problems on the court. FEAR, ANGER and LOSS OF CONCENTRATION. They may manifest in various ways, such as choking or nervousness, but fundamentally we are dealing with just those three problems. Loss of concentration is of course in itself not an emotion, but it is usually caused by emotions.

Of these emotions, the most difficult to deal with is fear in its various forms. We all know them by name: *choking, rubber arm, match nerves, tentativeness*. Some players go through their whole careers without ever coming to grips with fear. These are the types of players who might be absolute masters in practice, but fail to deliver in matches when it really matters. They also tend to be the main cause behind coaches' gray hair (joke).

Anger is the next in line as a destructive emotion. It too has variations: anger at self for mistakes, anger at umpires, anger at conditions, anger at audience and so forth. Anger too—just like fear—can be very destructive and break down one's game completely. Especially if one fails to get back into just focusing on the now. This varies wildly from player to player. Some seem to be able to get over it instantly (like McEnroe who almost played better after an angry outburst, while the opponent stood there all shaken). Others seem to carry on with the emotion for the rest of the match and lose (Kyrgios, at times).

Third in line is apathy, or as it's called in tennis: *tanking*. It means giving up or just playing badly on purpose. It's usually resorted to as a "solution" to avoid failure. The logic seems to be "If I don't try then I can't fail." At higher levels tanking is very seldom a problem (perhaps because according to the rules a player can be fined for not trying his or her best).

Finally we have something that, as we said, is not really an emotion in itself, but tends to be driven by emotions. I am talking about a LOSS OF FOCUS or attention; drifting off in one's mind, away from the present and instead thinking about the past or future or other places than the one where one is. It can be driven by anger, such as anger over a mistake one just made and can't stop thinking of. It can also be driven by positive emotions, such as elation at being close to winning and this emotion shifts one's attention to the prize ceremony, for instance. A worse situation is when fear of losing or choking drives attention to such past losses and thereby makes the present doubly worse.

Of course, there can be other emotional disturbances, but these are the most common. Even so, with relatively few emotional problems to deal with, a vast number of purported solutions have been invented to come to grips with them. With tennis being such a mental game (and, I might add, with so much money at stake) massive resources have been invested in trying to solve the problems. In fact, tennis was one of the first sports where sports psychology was developed.

Here is a review of some of these solutions and methods and my views on their effectiveness, ease of application and what specific difficulties they can be used for. There are obviously many other methods, but I have limited myself to some of the more common ones, those which in my view are the most (and least) effective. Some of the more effective ones I will devote separate chapters to, describing how they are done and how they should be used. Here we go, in no particular order.

First method. **Check if the problem is in fact technical**, and if so, solve that problem first. Many problems that are labelled mental are rooted in technical mistakes. I have sometimes heard coaches complain that their player "just isn't listening to them." They say they have told the player not to be so careful or hold back at important points or when trying to end points. Analyzing the situation more deeply, I have found that the real problem was that they lacked consistency. For instance, measuring their attempts at hitting winners (with an easy set up) they missed over half! Being cautious or nervous when hitting such a shot in a match situation is all but impossible to avoid and might in fact be considered a completely logical and rational reaction. So, check for other underlying problems before trying to remedy what is merely a mental symptom, not the real cause.

Seeing a mental coach. This can sometimes work. In my view it depends to a large degree on which mental coach one chooses and whether the methods he or she employs are the right ones for the player's problem. There is also the issue of compatibility. Is this someone you can trust and get along well with? If you try a certain mental coach and it does not seem to work: change!

Meditation, mindfulness, yoga and similar methods. These methods, if done correctly, are workable and helpful. Mostly they help with issues such as anger outbursts and improving concentration. But they can also be great tools for bringing about a general feeling of well-being and a healthier perspective on life. One way of getting started is to download many of the mindfulness apps that exist, perhaps followed by instructions from a teacher.

Changing your attitude about yourself. A later chapter, with the same title, describes how to do this. Basically the player takes more of a "coaching" attitude toward himself and thereby avoids much of the anger or self-blame that tends to occur after mistakes or after playing poorly

Rituals and routines. If you wonder what these words mean, take a look at a match with Nadal or Sharapova. Right before every point they go through the same motions, and in the case of Nadal the placement of beverages by his chair at side change is almost religiously precise. Sharapova usually goes to the back of the court, turns away and adjusts her strings. Another example is Djokovic who (almost obsessively) bounces the ball before serving sometimes. The more important the point, the more bounces. The question is whether these rituals fulfill any true purpose and help in any way. My view is that they can help to some degree with gathering focus ahead of the point and to more easily stay in the now. They can also help with visualizing what one wants to do next. I would categorize routines and rituals as a relatively shallow remedy. It might work with a player who does not have serious problems, and in any case is common in almost all sports. But it might not be a sufficient tool for handling more deeply rooted difficulties.

Re-framing. How you react to a certain situation or incident to a large degree depends on how you interpret it. And your interpretation in turn depends on the "framework". What we mean by that is perhaps best explained by an example. If you for instance are talking in front of a large crowd, and somehow say something stupid causing the audience to laugh at you, then normally you might get a feeling of embarrassment. But not necessarily. If prior to the talk you made a bet with someone that you could get the crowd to laugh at you, then the incident would trigger positive feelings. To take an even more obvious example: if you have the goal of hitting a winner in tennis and the ball goes out, you might feel disappointed. If, on the other hand, you were having a practice session and the coach had told you to hit the ball out, then doing so would make you feel successful. The "frame," as a term, describes your expectancy, your goals, the circumstances, etc. Changing your frame can have a profound effect on your emotions on a tennis court. It is one of the more effective, and also one of the easiest, methods to use for handling unwanted emotions. It can be done by the player himself, or with the help of a coach or mental trainer. I have limited myself to just briefly describing the term here and later on will devote a full chapter to it.

Exposure. I once took on a short-term job of painting metal roofs on tall buildings. To do this I had to stand near the edge of sharply slanted roofs 6 or 8 stories up! As I'm sure you can imagine my legs were shaking quite a bit and I had a strong feeling of vertigo (almost to the point of nausea). It's interesting how similar the feeling of vertigo is to the feeling of choking in a tennis match by the way. Your legs don't seem to work, your body shakes, your heart beats, and you might feel a cold sweat. After a few weeks of doing this every day the vertigo gradually went away and I could perform the job without any negative reactions. The same principle applies in tennis. Choking or nervousness tend to go away with sufficient exposure to match play – especially, important matches. This method of dealing with unwanted emotions is quite effective. Even though it is effective it can be a bit hard to apply. Opportunities to play important matches do not come every day. Chances are if you have a problem with nerves, you normally get knocked out early on in tournaments, so you get only one or two matches a week—not enough to achieve the effects of exposure.

CBT (cognitive behavioral therapy) is one of the more common tools applied by psychologists. It has the definite advantage of being one of the methods in psychology that has been scientifically proven to produce results. Additionally, it is not too hard to learn and could potentially be applied by the player himself or by the coach. Often the practitioner of CBT will do a few sessions with the "patient," then formulate a plan for what the patient (player) should do by himself. To a large degree it could be described as common sense. If, for instance, you tend to get overly angry the program could be to keep track of your anger and "measure" it on a scale from 1 to 10 and then work on lessening the outbreaks. There are good books on the subject, but perhaps the best route to take is to first see a professional and then work out how to be self-sufficient with applying it. In some cases the method might not be sufficiently effective though. This is especially true when there is a major underlying problem, such as a childhood trauma. In such cases a deep analysis may be required, getting to the actual source of the problem.

Deep analysis. With deep analysis we get down to the fundamental source of the problems, and by that I mean the fundamental source within the player's mind. It's an advanced procedure and needs considerable skill to apply. At the same time you could say it is the ultimate remedy if all else has failed, and highly effective when done right. It works on deep-seated emotions which nothing else seems to reach. The method is described more in detail in the chapter "Getting to the Source".

Winning. When it comes to building confidence and shattering fear or nervousness, nothing can replace winning. This is the Holy Grail of maximizing one's skills in tennis. With winning comes confidence and with confidence comes the ability to hit freely and letting go of all internal stops one might have. This is so much true that I often witness players trying to handle their various mental problems with the philosophy of playing lots of tournaments in the hope that things will eventually "click" by virtue of getting enough wins. It is certainly true that if one wins enough then confidence is sure to improve, which in turn will result in more winning. On the other hand it could be said that this philosophy is a little like trying to get rich by winning the lottery. My advice: by all means try to build confidence by winning and playing lots of matches. But at the same time don't take it so far that you neglect setting aside enough time for practice. Remember, one of the main reasons a player feels uncertain or lacks confidence is that he or she has not yet reached a sufficiently high level of consistency. Long and intensive practice is needed to build this. Furthermore, winning will not necessarily cure tendencies to get angry or losing focus. Therefore, even when one wins and feels confident, it is beneficial to devote time to improving one's mental skills.

Willpower training. The word willpower is almost synonymous with the traditional concept of mental toughness. Most people don't realize that willpower can actually be trained. A later chapter describes how.

Grow bigger/re-define the game. The basic idea here is to "grow bigger" than the various obstacles that tend to trigger negative emotions. The chapter "Be prepared to Double Up" describes it in more detail.

Concentration drills. There are many methods for increasing concentration and focusing skills. In fact, one very effective example is the drill described in the chapter *Consistency Training*. Being able to concentrate is a very basic and useful skill, and it has a general positive impact on many of the common mental and emotional problems in tennis

Visualization. We saw an example of this technique in a previous chapter, where basketball players visualized free throws and thereby improved their score almost as much as those who physically trained. You mind is a powerful tool, and visualization helps you mobilize it. A later chapter describes the method in detail. It can be very effective and has helped many athletes, especially in track and field events. What is it that a pole-vaulter does for so long before starting? You got it: visualize.

Converting negative energy to positive. This involves doing exactly what it says. If the player manages to do it, the method can be very workable. Especially in changing angry outbursts and other such reactions to something positive.

In the next few chapters we will go over in detail how some of the above-mentioned methods work and how to use them. I have chosen the techniques I have found most useful and which the reader will be able to apply without a tremendous amount of prior knowledge.

CHAPTER 19

CHANGE YOUR ATTITUDE TO YOURSELF

HERE is a little experiment. Find a tennis ball. Put it down in front of you and look at it. Now close your eyes and think about the tennis ball. Then open your eyes again.

What was that all about?

The experiment is designed to make you look at and consider something you may not have thought about before:

The ball is part of the physical universe around us. So is your body. When you thought about the ball, the picture of it was in your mind, obviously. Not in the physical universe. Now to the big question: who was looking at the picture? I'm sure your answer is "me." But who is me? It can't be your body, since the eyes were closed, right? Could it be your mind? No, since you could look at the ball it could not at the same time BE you. After all, if you can see it, it must be outside *YOU*. Rather strange when you start thinking about it.

Clearly there is "something" that looks at things in your mind and which also can put them there. It is the thing we ultimately refer to when we say that "*I* was the one looking at it". This *something* is not your body and is not your mind, or the pictures in your mind. It is also not your emotions or thoughts. Yet, it surely exists. How do we know? Because we know and can experience it.

Trying to explain this is something philosophers and science has struggled with forever. No clear answers have emerged yet. Some would say it is our soul. Others might say it is a collection of neurons creating this phenomenon somehow. But whatever the explanation, it is definitely something we all can experience and feel for ourselves, and that is all that really matters as far as we are concerned and as far as it applies to tennis.

Putting it another way: the body, the mind and the thoughts in our minds, are all examples of something we HAVE, not what we fundamentally, at the core, ARE. In daily conversation when we use the words "me" or "I" we include in them the whole package: body, mind, thoughts – everything. But using the word in the narrower meaning as described above can be very useful in improving your mental game in tennis. Here is how.

If you were, for instance, a formula 1 race car driver, there would be no doubt that the car is something you HAVE and not something that you ARE. Likewise, if you are a jockey, the horse is something that you HAVE, not something that you ARE. This distinction makes a difference in how you treat these things. If the car performs poorly (say, the brakes are not working properly) you would not say to yourself "I suck today." Or if the horse has a bad leg that day you would not get angry at the horse and kick it or yell at it. Instead you would try to fix those problems in a constructive way.

When it comes to tennis we so thoroughly identify with our bodies and minds that if the body performs badly we say "I suck" or some words to that effect. We get angry. We mentally kick ourselves. We can get so engaged in these emotions and complaints that we fail to do anything constructive about them, and in fact make the situation much worse. First we have a malfunctioning body, then we end up having a mind that is a mess and maybe even broken equipment or a point penalty for misconduct!

If instead we think of our body and the mind as something we HAVE, sort of like a race car or a horse, we can change our attitude. Be positive and constructive when something doesn't work, and not think of it as "me." We can take a bird's eye view of the situation. Notice exactly what is not working and try to fix it. We can be like a benevolent and positive coach who encourages and fixes things when they go wrong.

Treat your body, and even your mind, as if it were a horse or a car. Be understanding when things don't work as they should. Don't think of it as yourself but as something you have responsibility for; something valuable in your charge that you need to take care of in the most positive, constructive and effective manner.

If you succeed in this, you will soon find that you no longer have angry outbursts or self-blame when things don't work. You fix the problem.

CHAPTER 20

RE-FRAMING

MENTAL (emotional) reactions usually occur as a result of events in the environment. But not always, and not necessarily. It all depends on how you interpret the events and how you think about them (the frame). As a case in point, take the TV series *"The Dog Whisperer."* If you haven't seen it, it's about dog trainer Cesar Millan. Each episode features one or several particularly difficult, misbehaving dogs. The owners are usually desperate, displaying emotions ranging anywhere from grief and hopelessness to frustration and anger. And Cesar? Well, he is happy as can be. The more difficult the case, and the more distraught the owners, the happier he is. He just loves solving difficult cases. So it's not the dog *per se* that causes the unpleasant emotions. It's the dog's behaviour *combined* with how the owners think about it. To them it is an unsolvable problem. To Cesar it is an opportunity. At the end of each show the owners have always changed their attitude/emotions and learned something new. As Cesar puts it: "I don't train dogs. I train the owners and I help the dogs."

What can we learn from this? The emotions you feel about a certain situation totally depend on your thoughts and interpretation of it. The owners have interpreted it as a huge problem and react accordingly. Caesar Milan has interpreted it as an opportunity and a fun challenge and reacts with the proper emotions for this, such as excitement and cheerfulness. The situation itself has no "inner" significance or emotion built into it. The reaction all depends on how you think about it. We call this the FRAME. Depending on how you frame a situation, which is to say which context you place it in, your reactions to it will vary widely.

Here is another example. The situation of having a small yellow furry ball land on a certain white line or alternatively 2 cm outside this line does not, in and of itself, carry any emotional significance whatsoever. Yet, it can lead to the most violent outbursts. *"You cannot be serious, man! You cannot be serious!!! That ball was on the line! Chalk flew up...."* Well, you know the rest.... The frame, in this case, is that the match is tremendously important and every call matters. Furthermore (part of the frame) is that at that time it was possible for umpires to be wrong. There was no Hawkeye. The conclusion by the player is that he is being done in by the umpire; that it is all unfair; and that yelling would somehow better this situation. Possibly there is even a long past making itself known. Perhaps a cultural environment where it is normal to have an outburst if someone else gets in one's way and that this might override the importance of staying calm in a match situation.

How could this have been framed differently, and what might the emotional reaction have been then? Imagine a strange scenario where the actual competition was all about who could better handle wrong line calls, especially the most outrageous ones. And every time a player successfully managed to meet such a call with calm and dignity, he would be awarded a point. How would the player react to a blatantly incorrect line call? Probably with very positive emotions. I know, a pretty far-fetched frame, but it serves to illustrate the point that depending on the frame, the resulting emotions and reactions will vary all the way from very negative to strongly positive.

How can we apply these ideas realistically in tennis?
Why look at a match as a matter of life and death? Why not look at it as a beautiful opportunity? Or maybe a chance to diagnose what you need to work on? Or perhaps a chance to show for others your mental prowess and ability to "meet with Triumph and Disaster"? This method can be VERY effective. One important requirement, in order to apply it well, is to have a skilled coach who the player can trust and who is

able to create an "aura" of positiveness and confidence. Some of the world's best coaches have a fantastic ability to do just this. From my time working with Peter Lundgren I clearly witnessed his ability in this area. And from talking to players coached by Magnus Norman I learned (and could observe) his superior ability to create calm and confidence in his players. Sometimes this is the main added ingredient an otherwise well-trained player needs to reach higher levels.

If a situation tends to bother you, try re-framing it in a positive way.

CHAPTER 21

DEEP ANALYSIS— GETTING TO THE SOURCE

IF YOU CAN GET TO the basic, underlying, source of your problems of destructive emotions, your chances of handling them greatly improve. We know from previous chapters, that the true source of your (irrational) emotional reactions is not the things that the environment presents to you per se, but rather how you think about them. This mind-set and attitude often has its root much earlier in time than the present, and because of this they can be immensely difficult to change. They can go as far back as when you started playing tennis, or even earlier. And, boy, can these thoughts be sticky! To use an analogy, it is like when you first start up a new computer and you get to select what language to use. Whatever you choose will stick with that computer from here on out. But knowing how this mechanism works, we can use our knowledge to effectively undo the destructive emotions.

As an example of how this can take place in tennis, I once worked with a player who was extremely anxious about winning. Especially in matches where he was "supposed to win." This, of course, affected his playing very negatively, resulting in losses in matches that should not have been a problem at all. Attempts to change his attitude about the game and not be so deadly serious

about it proved impossible. No matter how hard he tried, those feelings remained. Tracing them back to the source we found that as a little boy he had been quite insecure and had a low selfimage. Then he started playing tennis, and for the first time received admiration and respect from others (he had a lot of natural talent). So he concluded that the best—or only—way to "be someone" in life was to win at tennis. His whole career was in many ways built around this basic idea, although he never actually thought about it in a conscious way. Well, as long as he was winning (which was just about all the time) he felt great about himself and the game. But then, as he reached higher levels, he started to run into opposition and started experiencing losses. These losses, of course, shook his confidence, and with it came various emotional reactions. Since his entire existence as a valuable, admired person hinged on winning in tennis, any risk of a loss, especially to a lower-ranked player, was on a subconscious level equated with a life-threatening attack to his very being. Of course, from that perspective, the appropriate emotional response would be extreme anxiety. How else should one react when one's life is in danger?

Analyzing this and looking at the original thoughts behind this whole situation, it became quite obvious that this way of thinking about his tennis was neither logical nor workable. If any risk of a loss equates to a threat to your life, we don't have to wonder about why the emotions become so strong and hard to control.

Part of this situation was also that his father had been a tennis pro, but never reached the very highest levels in the game. This put even further pressure on the player to perform.

Realizing all this, the player was now able to let go, and thereby change his emotions. He built a new career (actually, as it turned out, in a different sport), received a great sponsor deal and within a short time was ranked number one in his country and rose to a top international ranking.

What can we learn from this?

Irrational/overpowering emotions often have their roots at a much earlier time in life. At this earlier time, the player knowingly or unknowingly made decisions or conclusions about tennis, or perhaps even life in general. These conclusions "stuck" so to speak, and in turn governed the emotional responses in later life since they provided a ready-made interpretation of situations in tennis. Based on the earlier, ready-made conclusions, later emotional responses became inevitable, and indeed from that perspective not irrational at all (which is why they were so hard to change).

The rock bottom problem, and where everything went off the rails, is the original conclusion.

The solution is to thoroughly dig up, expose, and analyze this original conclusion. When seen clearly in hindsight, the irrationality and unworkability of it can be revealed. When this is realized, changing one's perspective becomes possible, and with it the ability to change the irrational emotional responses. It is worth noting here that these original thoughts always seem to have some logic to them. "It seemed like a good idea at the time" as the saying goes. To fully erase these conclusions, it very much helps to discover this underlying logic, and to then, by further analysis, realize how this was an error of judgement. Now the player is truly free to let go and to adopt a more workable viewpoint on his tennis and life.

The process described above is probably the most powerful tool of all for changing and coming to grips with irrational emotions. It has a major drawback though: it is not that easy to do. The earlier conclusions (and the situations in which they were made) are often heavily suppressed and hidden deep in one's mind. This is because they often were formed during moment of distress or other forms of trauma, and who wants to think of things like that? Our usual response is to do everything in our power to try to forget. It may, therefore, require expert help to dig them out and expose them. A skilled coach might be able to accomplish this. But, if not, expert help might be necessary.

CHAPTER 22

WILLPOWER TRAINING

If you can force your heart and nerve and sinew
To serve your turn long after they are gone,
And so hold on when there is nothing in you
Except the Will which says to them: 'Hold on!'
From the poem "If" by
Rudyard Kipling

WILLPOWER is very much part of what is called mental toughness in tennis. The two terms are almost interchangeable. Willpower means being able to push through and persist on a given course even when you don't "feel like it". Or to resist doing something which you intensely feel like doing, but which you know down deep is not good. If you feel like screaming out loud and breaking your racquet, but manage to resist the temptation, that's will power. If you are dead tired and every muscle and bone in your body tells you to give up, and yet you keep going, that's willpower. If you have been overpowered by your opponent and everything looks completely hopeless and you just want to quit, and yet you keep trying your very best until the last ball, that's will power.

Willpower makes it possible to keep going towards your actual long-term goals and not be swayed by emotions that don't help you get there. It makes it possible to keep training daily, even if it might be boring or painful some days, or if you'd rather be at the movies or watch TV. It makes it possible to keep a healthy diet, even if you'd rather be eating burgers, coke and ice cream.

Feelings and emotions (as we have covered earlier in the book) tend to push us around. Both toward doing things we know we really shouldn't be doing and toward not doing the things we should. Take people who are heavy smokers. We often hear such persons say, "I could easily quit if I just wanted to." Probably so. But what they are really saying is that they are not able to overcome their feeling of wanting to smoke, and so never actually "want" to quit. Down deep they surely are aware of the need to quit and what extreme danger they are putting themselves in. The word "want" has simply become synonymous with "feel like." The same thing applies to tennis players. They sometimes end up doing things they perfectly well know are destructive, but despite this are unable to resist the emotions compelling them in a non-optimum direction. Who could possibly be unaware of the fact that expressing anger at umpires, surroundings or even at themselves, is not desirable or something that forwards their game? Yet they do so. Why? Well, one reason is that their willpower is not strong enough to control the emotions.

Here is the good news though: willpower is in many ways just like muscles. Willpower can be trained and improved. And it turns out it's not that difficult. Here is a simple drill that goes a long way in strengthening willpower.

WILLPOWER DRILL

1. Get yourself a small notepad or calendar book.

2. Start collecting daily points and mark how many you get each day

3. The point system works as follows. Every time you do something that you don't "feel like" doing you get a point. Also, every time you resist doing something you "feel like" doing you get a point. In short, every time you overcome inner resistance you get a point. Example: doing the dishes even though you didn't feel

like it. Example: resisting throwing the racquet even if you felt like it. Example: resisting showing disappointment or anger over a missed shot even if you felt like it. Example: going running an extra mile even though you didn't feel like it. Example: taking a cold shower even though you really didn't feel like it. You get the idea.

4. An important point, of course, is that the things you do or resist doing should not in themselves be destructive. Needless to say, you would not choose things to do "even though you don't feel like it" such as committing a crime or violating your training schedule. Preferably the things you get points for would be things that enhance your long-term goals.

The drill will only work if the things you get points for are done on your own initiative and not because someone else told you or even encouraged you. The whole idea is that without any pressure or encouragement from others, you manage to overcome your inner resistance or urges.

Within a short time after starting this drill you will notice your inner resistance gradually giving up, so to speak, and you will gain control over the emotions that have interfered with your longterm plans and real purposes you have. You may also notice that various things you have been doing are not at all what you really want.

The drill can be very effective in tennis especially for things like:
- Resisting emotional outbreaks
- Not reacting negatively to one's mistakes
- Avoiding negative emotions or loss of energy after such things as having lost a set or having one's serve broken
- Being able to keep fighting no matter how tired the body feels

- More intensity in physical training as well as regular training sessions
- Resisting the urge of letting thoughts drift from the present

The drill is effective for handling the situations above but has some limitations. Match nerves and lack of confidence is better handled by other methods. Nevertheless, this drill is very easy to start without outside coaching or guidance and gives ample results in a short amount of time.

Try it!

CHAPTER 23

PETER'S METHOD

Peter Lundgren

THE LOSS against Glenn Layendecker in Australian Open 1991 (described in the chapter Mental Meltdown) was not the only time I endured that kind of painful experience. It had gotten a bit better over the years and I no longer reacted as strongly over losses. Earlier in my career I just got furious. One example was back when I played on the satellite tour. I was serving for the match and the tournament. I really wanted to win. But the same thing happened. I got careful, and suddenly the opponent broke back and went on to win the match. I just exploded and ran into the locker room, shattering my racquet into a thousand pieces and refused to come back out to the prize ceremony. After a while of me moping and being angry, tournament director Alan Mills (tournament referee for the Wimbledon tennis championships from 1983 to 2005) comes into the locker room and orders me in a rather firm voice to COME OUT! NOW! I did, and I apologized and had to pay a fine. Not my best moment in tennis....

In retrospect I can see that the common denominator was a momentary mental lapse (becoming careful or tentative, "playing safe") which then changed the momentum of the match and eventually resulted in defeat. I knew I had to come up with some sort of solution. The problem was clearly that I pulled back and became tentative in critical situations—not at all my natural style of playing.

What I came up with was this. I realized what triggered the whole reaction was my *thinking*. Instead of looking at the situation as an opportunity I started having thoughts like "what if he breaks me now" or "I better make sure I don't lose this." The emotional reaction connected to and caused by these thoughts was automatically fear. Fear of losing, fear of being broken, worry about my shots and so forth. All triggered by putting my attention on the negatives and the risk. The "what if..." of the situation. The thoughts had to change. What could I think instead? Just not caring about the situation did not work. Trying to imagine that there was no risk didn't work either. The method (or "trick," if you want to call it that) was to realize that the opponent is under just as much pressure as me. I would think to myself:

OK, he is under pressure now. He has the problem of trying to break me. I know I usually hold serve, so he will have a really hard time of it. The pressure is on his side of the net.

For me, this worked. And similar methods, or versions thereof, worked for other players as well. With Safin, for example, when he met Federer in AO, he was all nervous about meeting his idol. He was pretty convinced that he didn't have a chance (and the audience and the press were likewise convinced before the match). But I knew differently. I told him that I KNEW for a fact (which I did) that Roger had just as much respect for, or even fear of, Safin as vice versa, and that he definitely had a good chance if he just played his game freely and without hesitation. I told him that Federer was under pressure while he himself had absolutely nothing to lose or to prove. Well, it must at least to some degree have worked because he played incredibly well. And the rest is history.

Next case in point. Federer against Sampras. Wimbledon. Almost a copy of the example above. Federer was nervous and didn't think he had much of a chance. My talk to him: I knew Sampras had a lot of respect for him and Roger had the weapons to match Sampras. He just needed to play his game and not hold back. Again, the rest is history.

Give it a try!

CHAPTER 24

BE PREPARED TO DOUBLE UP

IMAGINE you are a boxer and you have been scheduled for a fight against an opponent of slightly higher ranking. Ahead of the match you prepare as best you can. You study the opponent's strengths and weaknesses. You get ready for getting hit (as you always will in a match), and for the physical effort the fight will take, sort of building a mental shield against the difficulties and pain you will face. You know it will be hard, but you are ready for it.

As the match is about to begin you are suddenly told that the fight has been completely changed. Instead of fighting the opponent you prepared for you are supposed to fight TWO opponents. Simultaneously! "But don't worry, they are ranked slightly lower than you," you are told. How would you react? My guess is that you would get pretty angry and most likely refuse the fight. Then again, if you were sufficiently confident in your skills and ability to beat both of them, you might take a deep breath, decide that you are bigger and better than both of them and accept the challenge.

Or how about this: You have a fight against a much lower-ranked boxer. Not much preparation needed. You are confident you will win. But then you are told just before the fight that you will have to fight with one hand tied behind your back. How would you react?

What, you may ask, does this have to do with tennis? Everything! Tennis players are subjected to these types of changes all the time. Let me explain.

When getting ready for a difficult task we prepare ourselves as much as possible. We make sure we have all the materials and equipment needed. And, most importantly, we prepare mentally. How? By playing out in our minds what might take place and what sort of obstacles or difficulties we might encounter. That way, when it happens, it doesn't impact so strongly upon us and we have a plan ready for dealing with it. Part of this process is that we sort of "calibrate" ourselves. How hard do I have to push? How big do I have to be? How much pain will I have to face? How long do I have to keep it up? In short, who do I have to be; what kind of person? How big, how strong?

The boxing examples above illustrate how hard it is to re-set the expectations and estimations of a future effort once it has begun. Re-calibrating is a very difficult task mentally, even harder than calibrating in the first place. The US military is quite aware of this. As part of training new recruits for tough outfits, such as the Marines or Navy Seals, you often see difficult tasks completed where the new recruits expect they are done for the day, only to find that an additional challenge has been added. So they rapidly have to adapt and re-define what it is they are trying to accomplish or else fail. Always be ready to double up. Always be ready for a new and tougher game, or that things don't turn out the way you expected.

In tennis we prepare for a match against the opponent. We expect and prepare for a tough battle. We calibrate how tough we have to be, what effort we have to put out, what suffering we will have to endure. Then the match starts. Suddenly we discover that the match was not what we were prepared for. There is lots of wind, the umpire is (so we think) unfair and Hawkeye is malfunctioning, the court in in terrible shape and so forth. In short, the game we prepared for (a fair and normal tennis match) is not what we are facing. It is as if we suddenly have TWO opponents: the tennis player and all these other factors that we must contend with. All too often the reaction is anger or whining or protests. Only the mentally toughest players re-group and effectively deal with the obstacles.

Sometimes the problem is with ourselves. We have prepared for a match and assumed that our usual abilities and tools will work. But once the match starts, we discover to our dismay that the serve or some other shot is not working that day. Or perhaps we just don't see the ball like we usually do in practice. Perhaps we find that the racquet has been strung too tight or too loose and there is nothing we can do about it mid-match. So we have to play as if one of our arms were tied behind our back. How do we handle it? All too often the reaction is anger, broken racquets outbursts or maybe simply giving up. Only the mentally toughest players re-group and effectively deal with the handicap.

Failing to deal with what we may call a "changed game" results in only one thing: losing. Anger, complaining, throwing a tantrum, breaking racquets does not work. Sad but true.

The only thing that works is to rapidly adapt to the new circumstances; the new game, so to speak. How? Here are some tips. Make up your mind that you are bigger and more powerful than any challenge that can be thrown at you. So there is wind. OK, I can deal with that. Bad, unfair, umpire? No way I'm going to let such a little thing bring me down. Oh I see. The opponent is a lot better than I thought. Doesn't miss like usual. OK, I'll just play twice as good. He ain't seen nothing yet.

Connect with your inner power. Realize that you have a lot more to give, no matter how hard you already are trying. How fast could you run if a bear were chasing you? How focused would you play if your life and the life of your family depended on it? How clever would you be in finding solutions rather than whining?

Be ready to re-prepare if circumstances call for it. If you suddenly find yourself engaged in a completely different game than you had expected, be willing to accept this and just change your plans and preparation accordingly. A major part of this change is often the estimation of how big and powerful you have to be and how strong of an opponent (or opponents, if factors such as wind enter in) you are facing. Just say to yourself: OK, new game. I can be big enough to win that one too. BRING IT ON!

"Don't get mad, get even," as the saying goes. If you feel for instance that the opponent is using gamesmanship or is being unfair, don't waste time, energy and emotion on it. Just get even by playing better.

If some of your own tools don't work as you expected, be it your physical equipment, your body, your vision of the ball or something else, don't give up. First of all, realize that you have a different game to play than you planned for. Realize that it will be a challenge and probably more difficult than you anticipated. Now you really need to put your mind to solving a much more difficult task. How can you work around the difficulty? How can you compensate? Would running harder help? Focus on what CAN be done and do it. Then in time the difficulties may go away.

Worst-case scenario: none of the above works. Now what do you do? You try these and other solutions over and over and never lay down or give up. In the end if nothing has worked, well, then you lose. And you have to be willing to lose. That's part of the game. Everyone loses. But a loss is nothing to be ashamed about if you know that you did everything in your power to try and change it. If you "left everything on the court" then what else could you do?

The problem is that often players don't work constructively when faced with unforeseen circumstances. Instead they get angry or whine or even become destructive.

The true masters of the game deal with the challenge. That's one of the main differences between lower-ranked players and the top.

Start working on this and incorporate it into your practice sessions as early as possible. The habit of adapting to challenges and not bending to them can take some time to acquire, but is well worth the effort. Besides, the game will become more fun if you do so. Nothing more to get upset or angry about. How would that be?

CHAPTER 25

CONCENTRATION DRILL

THIS IS PROBABLY the simplest drill you will encounter and at the same time one of the most powerful, if correctly done. It works to the degree that you honestly follow the instructions exactly as written.

The mind tends to behave like an unruly monkey and do whatever it wants to, with us having very little to say about it. The very first step in getting control over it is to get the monkey to sit still and stop chattering all the time. If we want to control our emotional reactions or stop our loss of focus in matches, then certainly we need to be able to do NOTHING. That's right: NOTHING.

Here is the drill.

1. Sit in front of a table in a regular kitchen chair without armrests. Place your hands in your lap. Legs straight down (not crossed).
2. Place a tennis ball on top of the table in front of you. Look at the ball and do NOTHING. Just be there.

Continue with the drill until you can sit comfortably looking at the ball for at least 30 minutes straight without moving around, without having to scratch, without falling asleep, and without having your thoughts wander.

It is OK to blink, but not nervously or in an exaggerated way.

You may feel various very unpleasant feelings, sensations and emotions. They will all dissolve if you just continue doing the drill.

You might go through the following stages:

- Tend to fall asleep
- Pain in various body parts

- Itching
- Boredom
- Laughing
- Your thoughts (the inner monkeys) chattering
- Reaching a final state of extreme presence and calm

Doing the drill for 30 minutes a day, it may take you several weeks to fully and honestly get through. It might be the toughest drill you have ever done.

CHAPTER 26

VISUALIZATION

"What the mind of man can conceive and believe, it can achieve."

Napoleon Hill
American author

VISUALIZATION basically means creating an inner picture or movie in your mind of something you want to bring about, such as how you will run a race or maybe how you will hit a ball in tennis.

Visualizing helps improve performance. We learned in a previous chapter about the experiment in which basketball players who merely visualized free throws improved almost as much as those who actually practiced. Visualization can also help calm nerves in critical situations. By focusing positively and visualizing what should happen, attention is removed from potentially negative outcomes so there is nothing left to be nervous about.

Visualizing was one of the favorite methods used by Magnus Norman as a player. In the beginning of his career, around age 18-19, he had been seeing a mental coach, but his methods did not fit with Magnus' needs. As he put it "I didn't like sitting there basically holding hands and looking at my childhood." So instead he started reading books about the mental game and applying what he learned. Visualization was one of the main methods. He started using it in matches and ahead of matches. Ahead of the match (like the night before) he would go through the match and anything that could happen so that he was prepared for it. He would also go through positive matches from the past, visualizing them. Then when the actual match took place, he would again go through positive scenarios at side changes. Part of this also entailed shutting out the noise of the present and the audience. He would just focus on this, and even sometimes put a towel over his head to shut out everything else that could possibly disturb his focus.

For Norman this worked quite well. He mentioned one time in Australia when the weather suddenly changed and the match had to be moved indoors. Mentally (by visualizing) he had prepared for this and could therefore handle it without a problem. Later on in his career, when he switched to coaching, he would have his players use similar methods. That's why you could sometimes see Robin Söderling putting a towel over his head at side changes.

There is much more to visualization though. As it says in the quote in the beginning of the chapter, what the mind of man can conceive and believe, it can achieve. If you want to get the most out of visualizing, just "seeing" that which you want to happen is not enough: all perceptions should be involved. Sounds, physical sensations, emotions, even smells. The more "real" the image the more impact it will have.

The method is not limited to physical activities though; it can also be used to develop mental abilities. If, for instance, there is a problem with nervousness (or choking) in matches, one could visualize a new, better and calmer version of oneself. The visualization could include situations where one would normally get nervous, but in the visualization one remains calm and confident.

Here is one more tip: to really turbo charge the visualization process, do not just think of what will be in the future, think of it as something that already exists. Let me explain. If we hypothetically pretend that you have magical abilities and that you can make anything you desire happen by merely wishing for it—sort of like a genie—well then you better be really careful about what you wish for. If you think and visualize that something "will happen one day" like, say, becoming rich and famous, it never will actually materialize. Why? Because the wish was placed in the future, and the future will never be now!

So you want to be confident? Visualize that you ARE confident, not that you will become confident in the future. So you want to get a better forehand? Visualize that it IS better (will all the perceptions and feelings that go with it) not that it will become so in the future.

The better you get at visualizing, the more impact it will have. And who knows, maybe one day you will get so good at it that you can affect reality at will! If that happened, what would you wish for?

Remember:

"What the mind of man can conceive and believe, it can achieve."

CHAPTER 27

CONVERTING NEGATIVE ENERGY TO POSITIVE

A PLAYER I WAS COACHING had a problem with negative emotions raising their ugly head in matches. They would come up especially if he was making mistakes or if he was losing points he felt he was supposed to win. He would get angry, whine, criticize himself (often out loud so that the opponent could hear it) even throw his racquet sometimes. As if this wasn't bad enough, the situation would persist for a while and could even lead to losing the next point, game, set or match! He just wouldn't or couldn't let go.

The problem was also visible in practice. If, for instance, he failed at a certain drill, the reactions would surface (and be clearly visible to one and all watching). So we started working on finding a solution to this. The first thing he came up with was the idea of just "pretending," sort of playing theatre, making it look as if there was no reaction or as if everything was just fine. Meanwhile, on the inside, the negative emotions would continue in full force. This approach was definitely better than nothing, but didn't really handle the whole situation. The emotions would still affect the next few seconds or minutes of play in a negative way, so some further work was needed to resolve things. Next step was an attempt to, as he called it, "relax": take it easy or turn off the emotions. He managed to do so, but now an unintended consequence of turning things off happened. He no longer had the positive energy or drive that was needed to fuel his efforts in match play. In place of the negative emotions there suddenly was just nothing! This too, of course, affected his playing negatively. So back to the drawing board. What to do? What to do?

Converting Negative Energy To Positive

Then, during a practice session, a solution suddenly came to him. "I know, I can just convert the negative energy to positive energy!"

And it worked. After this the negative emotions both in practice and in match situations virtually disappeared. Nothing but a positive attitude and energy remained.

So how was it done? How did he manage to accomplish the conversion? I asked him, and he said he didn't know, he just did it somehow. Luckily, with some further probing he came up with an answer. He roughly followed the steps below:

I notice a reaction (anger, whining, etc.) but stop it before it takes over, no matter how much it burns inside.

I say to myself "the fact that I am reacting so strongly means that I really want to perform well. It is a sign that I care. And I know that I like tennis and I'm so happy to have the privilege to be able to play."

"Let's use that inner glow to make a positive energy. Let my inner power loose. Use it to play better".

It worked for him. I hope it can work for you, too.

CHAPTER 28

BAD DAYS

EVERYONE HAS THEM. Even the best of us. The question is how well you deal with them and how bad your worst level is, compared to your normal. The thing that defines the very best players is that they are extremely good at dealing with lows and even on their worst day, when nothing seems to work, they are still remarkably good and difficult to beat.

As the saying goes: the first thing to do when you find yourself in a hole is to stop digging! True enough, and never more so than in tennis. Many players tend to dig themselves deeper by complaining, getting angry, throwing or breaking their racquet, taking it out on linesmen or (worse) spectators, even sometimes hitting themselves with the racquet in despair, as if this would somehow change the situation.

Various factors can contribute to having a bad day. Some are obvious, others much less so. To begin with, if the body is hurt or somehow physically impeded, it will obviously impact the level of play. If the legs seem heavy or an arm hurts, it's very hard to play your best. Life around you can also impact play—an argument with your wife or girlfriend, for instance, or losing someone close to you.

Then there are nerves. A little tension can be good. But too much of it can completely ruin your play, as certainly and as devastatingly as having sprained your ankle.

The common denominator between all the above causes of bad playing is that they can be seen or otherwise perceived without too much trouble. Upsetting as they may be, you can at least know that they are there, and you can attempt to make the best out of the situation using any of the remedies suggested in this book.

There is one other thing, however, a hidden factor, a destroyer of game, hidden out of sight and unnoticed until it wreaks havoc. It is rarely talked about and often goes unnoticed, remaining a frustrating mystery to the player. "Why can I not hit the ball right today?"

It is quite possible to feel happy and harmonious, feel that the body is in perfect shape, feel confident—not nervous—about the upcoming match, feel that you have practiced hard and all your shots are working well and still, once you step out on the court discover to your dismay that your shots are not working. No matter how hard you try, the ball just flies, and you can't seem to figure out why.

The hidden factor is what's sometimes known as "hand-eye coordination" or ball perception. In other words, how well you are seeing the ball. Players are often told by coaches to watch the ball. While this is necessary, it does not really define clearly what it is that should happen, so a brief explanation is in order.

There are lots of different styles in tennis. Lots of variations in how the ball is hit. One-handed backhand, two-handed backhand, lots of top spin, flat shots, serve-and-volley and so on. There is no single way, that is always "the right way," to hit the ball, which works for everyone all the time.

But there is one aspect of how to hit the ball that holds true for all players in all situations: it has to be hit in the sweet spot on the racquet. And in order to do that, the player has to know where the ball will be before it gets there (since the swing of the shot has to be started before the ball arrives). In other words, the player has to be able to very precisely predict the trajectory of the ball, both where it will be in space and exactly when it will be there. This is what is usually referred to as hand-eye coordination. It is also called timing—which is really just another way of saying that the player knows WHEN the ball will reach a certain point in space.

This ability is very well developed in all good tennis players. There really is no exception. With the best players, for instance, you can see how they sometimes catch a serve (maybe it was out) right on their racquet. I mean the ball just sits there, as if it had been caught in a glove. This requires incredibly precise timing and certainty of where the ball will be. Yet most top players can perform this trick effortlessly. This is the ability I am referring to when I talk about timing or hand-eye coordination.

Now a question: how does it feel to have good timing/handeye coordination? Is there a noticeable, special, feeling you have in your hand or eyes or other part of your body that tells you that you have good timing that day? The answer is "no." There is no particular feeling associated with this. You pretty well know when your body is in good shape and you definitely know when you have no pain or other problems with your body. You also know when you feel happy and harmonious, or when you feel confident and not nervous. But timing and hand-eye coordination remains out of sight until you step out on the court. Then it makes itself known in no uncertain terms. And it is quite possible to feel fantastic, and yet be way off, or the opposite: you feel quite bad, but discover to your surprise that your shots work magnificently.

I would venture to say that this factor, above all others, is the one that tends to determine whether you will be having a bad or good day, or indeed be playing in the zone.

Hand-eye coordination is not, despite the name, an ability that resides in the hands. It is something in your brain. It has been programmed and enhanced through years of training until it becomes second nature. It has long been known to science that we do not actually have feeling inside the brain. It is, for instance, possible to perform brain surgery without anesthetics in the actual brain itself since we have no feeling there. Since hand-eye coordination resides in the brain we have no good way of knowing how well it will work on a given day other than just hitting the ball and checking it out. To make things worse, this ability tends to fluctuate a bit, and mostly so beyond our conscious control.

Bummer!

The best we can do is to try to create the most favorable conditions possible to help maximize the ability in matches. Regular practice routines help. Being in great physical shape tends to help a lot. Anything that improves oxygen uptake in the brain helps. A healthy diet helps. Meditation and similar practices can help. Making sure to have a supportive and harmonious environment helps.

Finally, and perhaps most importantly, realize that hand-eye coordination is something that is almost impossible to control by your own volition. It is not your fault, and it does not mean that you suck (as some players tell themselves when it happens). Be willing to accept the natural fluctuations.

When, and if, you have a day when your timing is off, recognize it as soon as possible, and do whatever you can to improve your odds. Run faster. Make very sure NOT to "dig a deeper hole" for yourself. Sometimes things improve after a while into the match if you just do your best.

CHAPTER 29

WAWRINKA VS FEDERER

Stockholm Open 2010

Here is a story that illustrates several of the subjects we have covered in the book. First of all exemplary "master coaching" ahead of the match; second, an example of not getting down on yourself when you're behind; third, evidence of the importance of consistency, and finally how even the smallest negative thought can completely change the momentum of a match.

Peter Lundgren

OCTOBER 2010. STOCKHOLM OPEN. Wawrinka was meeting Federer in the quarter finals. He was 1-5 in head-to-head ATP matches against Roger. Although he had been playing well during the year up to that point, his confidence was low ahead of the match.

As a coach I firmly believe there is a time to talk and a time to be silent. Some players prefer to work out things on their own and take their time. Others need a boost and some live communication. With players at the very highest level there isn't really that much you can say before a match. They already have their game and you will not be able to change anything major at the last minute. So it mostly comes down to mental factors and inspiration ahead of the match. This is particularly true when playing someone like Roger Federer. He knows all the tricks. He has no particular weaknesses you can exploit (unless you can hit about a million perfect backhands in a row). He has all the weapons to counteract whatever sneaky ideas you can come up with. There is really only one strategy (if you want to call it that): let loose. Play your best all the time. Don't hesitate. Keep this up constantly and for the entire match. That's your only chance of winning. On one hand a pretty overwhelming proposition. On the other hand sort of a relief. You've got nothing to lose and can just relax and let it rip—win or lose.

It was quite evident that Wawrinka felt pretty down and desolate thinking about the upcoming match. He was heading for a loss and this was definitely a time when some inspiration was necessary.

I asked him what his thoughts were about the match. He said, in so many words, that he didn't think that he could take more than a few games, and with Roger's devastating upper hand at their previous meetings (5-1) he was quite convinced he wouldn't stand a chance. He had sort of accepted defeat before the match had even started.

So how do you respond to that as a coach? What can you even say? I had to dig down myself and try to look at it. Did he actually have a chance? Could I see a way he could win? How? What weapons did he have? Was there anything he was better at than Roger? Was there a way he could dominate him? When you try to make a player see how he could win it's important that you actually believe and can "see it" yourself. You have to be brutally honest or lose your credibility. Well, fortunately I could see a way, and I fully believed it. This is what I told Stan:

Stan I have seen you play. I have seen what you can do. You have incredible power on both sides, forehand and backhand. And when you let it loose, and make it work, there is NO ONE, and I really mean that, NO ONE who can stand up against you. Not even Roger. You need to let all hesitation go and just let out your inner beast. Don't let Roger pull you into long rallies. You will not win that way. Just let it rip whenever you can and use your strength without any doubts or reservations.

I could see Stan knew I was right, and he visibly brightened up. Yeah, that's what he was going to do win or lose, he was not going to go down holding back.

How did it go?

First set. Stan played incredibly, firing on all cylinders. And as usual when he plays like that, he blows through any and all resistance. The set ended 6-3 with not one but TWO service breaks for Stan. Impressive. The crowd was beginning to smell an upset in the works.

Second set. Wawrinka breaks early and is up 2-0. At 3-1 he has even one more chance to break, but Federer serves up an ace and manages to hold. Then, with Stan serving, he starts having some minor whispers of thoughts going through his head. *What if Roger manages to come back? What if he breaks me now?* So Stan (consciously or subconsciously) became slightly careful. Not as a strategy. But those tiny fragments of thoughts were enough to trigger emotions of fear which trigger holding back…well, you know how it goes. No matter how well you know the strategy and what you should do from a logical perspective, your physical performance inevitably changes.

Against an opponent like Federer this is a sure-fire ticket to losing. And sure enough, it all came down to a single point. I don't remember if it was a missed passing shot or something else, but that one point gave Roger the tiniest of openings, and as usual, he wiggled out from his losing situation in the match, came back and in the end won 2-6, 6-3, 6-2.

Roger has this uncanny ability to find a tiny hole to escape through when things are the most pressing. Even though it might look like a hopeless situation, he keeps coming at his opponent, never getting down on himself and not lowering his performance (although, I might add, this was not something he was born with but had to develop over time when he was younger).

Wawrinka was quite devastated and sad after the loss. He had been so close to winning. But this point…no, not even this point, this *tiny thought*, this *fraction of a thought* of hesitation had been all it took to completely change the momentum and seal the fate of his match.

It's interesting to notice how the very best in tennis seem to have this ability to turn seemingly impossible situations around. How do they do it? How is it possible? I think there are two main reasons. First of all, they do not let difficult situations get to them. They keep plugging away at it, trusting that it might turn around and that they, sooner or later, will get a chance. That's definitely one reason they can do it. The other one has to do with consistency. When you face a player like Federer, Nadal, Djokovic or (a name from my era) Jimmy Connors, you know that they are never ever just going to "give it to you." I remember from my own career, meeting Jimmy Connors, that even serving at 40 – 0 you did not feel safe. Against any other player you could relax a bit. But if you did that against Jimmy he would immediately grab the chance and come back at you. Suddenly it would be deuce and then he might break. The best simply make fewer mistakes than other players. Their lowest level is still incredibly high regardless of how much pressure they are under. To a spectator it might appear as if they always seem to get lucky when it really matters. In reality, it comes from long hours of hard practice. Or as Arnold Palmer once famously put it:

It's a funny thing, the more I practice the luckier I get.

CHAPTER 30

REACHING THE ZONE

In the beginning of the book we talked about playing in the zone, what it means and how this would be the ultimate goal of mental tennis.

We have now arrived at the final chapter and we shall try to deliver on our promise, deciphering how to get there.

There is a strange thing about playing in the zone: it can (and does) happen at any level of the game. You would think that only the best players experience it, but not so. Even beginners can sometimes feel they reach the zone. This means that it is not just about how well you play from an absolute, objective standpoint, but some sort of inner phenomenon. What follows are some of my own opinions and thoughts about what the zone is.

There are two definite phenomena that characterize the zone. The first of them is a feeling of inner calm and harmony. Your mind is quiet, and you can "just let go," as Federer put it. This state of mind can be achieved with a high degree of certainty if the drills in chapters *Consistency Training* and *Concentration Drill* are done correctly and for long enough. Then, to get to the same mental state in matches, it is necessary to deal with and master all the various type of distractions that tend to shake and disturb it. The main one is negative emotions, such as those covered in Part Three of the book. The mental state of being in the zone can be achieved with a high degree of regularity. It helps with the physical playing level as well, since the mind is not interfering (as described in the chapters on emotions) in that performance is not distracted.

The other phenomenon that characterizes playing in the zone is that the physical performance level is above the usual. This can happen with or without the mental state mentioned above, although on the rare occasions when one's level is unusually high, the tendency is to let go and relax mentally as well, thereby approaching the mental side of the zone.

So the two sides, mental calm and physical performance, tend to affect each other and to take place at the same time. The heightened physical performance can be the harder of the two to control and bring about at will. Some days you just "see the ball better" without knowing why. Being calm and alert helps, but not always. We talked about this and what causes it in the previous chapter *Bad Days*.

Furthermore, just as the zone is *something* it is also (very much so) *nothing*! Being in the zone is a state of mind with absolutely no distractions or disturbances. Like an orchestra with all the instruments perfectly in tune. In that situation *any* of the instruments being even slightly out-of-tune will disturb the harmony. Such is also the case with playing in the zone. Everything seems in perfect tune. The body is in good shape and does not distract. The mind is calm and focused. The shots and how they are formed is automatic and needs no thought. It is like a clear glass of water. You can see through it with no distortions. The ball looks bigger and you simply cannot miss. Now, what would happen if at the bottom of this glass of water there was a little dirt or mud? As long as it did not get stirred up, no problem. But if anything caused it to get moved around the whole glass would become cloudy. Playing in the zone is when lots of positive things are happening and when *nothing* disturbs it. Suppose that something *does* disturb the calm (like a wrong line call or nervousness, for example). Your mind and your physical playing is then disturbed and distorted. What do players tend to do in that situation? STIR some more!

In order to get back to (or into) the zone, it is necessary to cultivate the ability to calm one's mind.

To sum things up: the zone can be described as a state of heightened abilities (most often, at least in tennis, caused by improved ball perception), accompanied by a state of *nothing*, where the mind is empty and there are no distortions or distractions in the mind or in the body.

We return to the question of how to get there. I suppose it would at least theoretically be possible to acquire the ability to turn it on at will. Some of the very top performers in sports seem to have succeeded in this. (For example, the previously mentioned discus thrower Al Oerter or the magnificent basketball player Michael Jordan).

For us mere mortals, the best we can do is to learn from the masters. Considerable research has been done in the field. There are some common denominators among "the best" and it's no great mystery what they do. Basically, a combination of ALL the various things we have mentioned in this book. Since the zone consists of many things working simultaneously in harmony, there is not one *single* magic trick that will immediately bring it about. The only question is whether you are willing to put in the long hours of hard work it takes to get there, and whether you are brave enough and insistent enough to discover and face up to your weaknesses. How bad do you want it? That's the main question.

With the drills in this book, and the knowledge that goes with them, you can definitely do it. At the very least you will experience playing in the zone more frequently than before, and you will be able to have mental balance almost all the time.

Then what?

This is not the end of the story. When it comes to reaching and playing in the zone there are degrees or levels you could say. The description above covers the level, or type, of "zoning" regularly encountered in sports: *playing above normal capacity, with confidence, focus and heightened awareness.* In very rare instances a person can reach even higher levels. The psychologist Abraham Maslow called it "peak experiences". The concept was originally developed in 1964, and Maslow describes peak experiences as *"rare, exciting, oceanic, deeply moving, exhilarating, elevating experiences that generate an advanced form of perceiving reality, and are even mystic and magical in their effect upon the experimenter."* It can indeed happen in sports, but is very rare.

My final word is this. The human mind has an ability to reach higher states. Experiencing the zone in tennis or any other sport, is simply a taste of this. An appetizer you could say. But an appetizer sometimes so powerful and profound that the "one moment in time" can live with a person for the rest of their lives. The zone, as described above, is not the main course though. Remember that.

Higher states are possible.

But beyond the scope of this book.

ACKNOWLEDGMENTS

I would like to thank some of the main people who contributed and helped bring about this book.

Peter Lundgren. First and foremost, of course. Peter contributed with interesting stories and examples from his own career as player and coach. He also shared his knowledge of the game and quality checked the information and advice in the book. Additionally, he has been an important support for me in the writing and served as a sounding board both for contents and readability.

Magnus Norman. Magnus let me interview him about the mental game and also helped with contacts to other top players who did the same. Mikael Tillström, Niklas Kulti, and Jonas Björkman, among others. During several years of collaboration with Good to Great tennis academy I had constant access to the players in the program, worked with some of them from time to time and sometimes had the opportunity to be on court with Magnus or his other talented coaches, observing how they worked.

Elias and Mikael Ymer, who had enough trust in me to let me coach them. I learned a lot from working with them, and hopefully they did to.

Daniel Windahl. A special thanks to Daniel Windahl for working with me on his mental game and having the courage to open up to others about how it helped.

Stefan Edberg who also let me conduct a long interview with him about the mental game and some of his insights after starting to coach Federer.

Ron Bernstein helped with marketing aspects of how the book was written.

Jonas Arnesen. Tennis journalist and writer for his immensely helpful feedback and advice with the overall disposition and readability of the book.

Acknowledgments

Lisa Mullenneaux. Helped with proofreading and text editing.

www.ingramcontent.com/pod-product-compliance
Lightning Source LLC
Chambersburg PA
CBHW052204090526
44583CB00015BA/1502